How to Make It in London

Ada Sytner

Clink Street

London | New York

There is no elevator to a career, you have to walk up the stairs
Emil Oesch

Contents

If you think you can, you're right.
If you think you cannot – well you're right.
Henry Ford

Since I can remember, I have always tried to prove my immediate surroundings that everything is possible. On contrary to popular beliefs and my own complexes I have assigned ambitious tasks and I have outdone myself. Why? Because we should do everything in our power to achieve financial and life satisfaction!

1
Introduction

*Confronted with the rock, stream always wins -
not because of its strength, but because of its perseverance.*
Buddha

I think that you will not find such a guidebook on the shelves at any bookstore or on the internet. Although it contains many typical guidebook chapters, it is not an abstract statement written by someone who is trying to advise people how to find a dream job, having no experience in this field, and without ever being in a similar situation. In this book, among other things, I devise my story about the fate of an immigrant and intricate career paths. If you are looking for a typical handbook on how to write a resume and prepare for an interview, you will find lots of them in bookstores. I have come a long way: from the seller in a store to a banker in the City of London, fighting with a lot of adversity, but above all with the restrictions that were embedded deep in my head.

This book is addressed to people who want to find better jobs. Many people dream of making a career only, not incorporating their desires into action. They lack self-confidence. They cannot find a stimulus to make a step forward. They do not know the English language well enough to feel confident while seeking their fortune abroad. Since Poland entered the European Union, much has changed. We are ambitious and hard-working people. We hold better and better positions previously reserved for the British only. I am very happy about this. There is enough space for everyone.

I still see that many Poles and other nationalities are still stuck in the same places of employment. For them, time has stopped. If they are satisfied with what they achieved – this book is not addressed to them. My story may be interesting for people who dream of a better life but feel the fear of the unknown and have no idea for the change. This handbook contains a variety of examples taken from real life. I will share with you my experiences and my friends'. We all have the same fears, concerns and problems. I do not hesitate to write about my personal struggles, because I think that the examples taken from life are priceless. I came to England not as a twenty-year-old girl, but as an experienced woman. I was thirty-one, I had family, and the conviction that if I did not begin to act soon, the time would fly through my fingers. The changes that took place soon in my life, occurred quickly and intensely. But do you have time? I think that regardless of age – there is never enough time. I do not even want to think what would happen if I came to London five or seven years earlier. The whole world would have been mine.

Probably, the fact the book was published in Polish and English does not surprise anybody. I would like to get to the widest possible circle of readers, even those who do not speak fluent English, especially to my fellow countrymen. For people who may need support and mentoring. I do not think that native inhabitants of Britain would need my guidance – and so they have a big advantage over us – especially the language, and because they often do not benefit from this, they have a lot to lose.

I admit that with this book I can somehow accomplish myself. I have always felt a compelling urge to advise and assist others, especially people who cannot make full use of their abilities and opportunities that life gives them. My comments and advice usually turned out to be accurate. Instead of being limited to advise only to a small group of friends, I decided to encourage many people to read this guide. I think, it will go into the hands of people who genuinely have decided to change something in their life and intend to follow this objective.

Most guidebooks focus on large steps and rapid promotion, but unfortunately this is only good for people who have already made a career and have an impressive track record. And what about those who have to make lots of small steps, starting from mastering of the English language to building their CV from scratch? For them I present in his book not only examples from my life and stories of my friends, but also practical tips on how to effectively learn English, how to raise qualifications, find a job, how to crash into the employment agency, how to perform a SWOT analysis, how to write a good CV, what questions will help to prepare for the interview. For determined readers, the guidebook includes a list of fifty work agencies in London.

It is a myth that to have a great job, we need to become perfectly fluent in English. In the book I reveal what most individuals do to learn it. Much to your surprise, it will be very simple techniques that really work.

In this book, I bring up a lot of important issues related to the achievement of financial balance and I answer questions which give sleepless nights to people dissatisfied with their life and who wait for their five minutes. I am going to convince you that most of the obstacles are easy to overcome and there are no such problems that cannot be solved.

2
What prompted me to write this book?

If there is a book you really want to read,
but has not been written yet, then you have to write it yourself.
Toni Morrison

What prompted me to write this book? There are a lot of answers to this question – you can find them in every chapter. To create the guidebook you are now reading, above all I was encouraged by observation of the immediate environment in London. I deal with people who came here long ago or recently, but most of them do not speak English, and only a few employ communicative English. After ten years since Poland entered the European Union there has still been reproduced the same stereotype. Girls are employed as babysitters and help in housework; guys work on construction sites for a ridiculous rates. It is sad how they are exploited by Polish or English employers.

Of course, I want to emphasise that no work dishonours anyone, and if someone is satisfied with their current profession, they perhaps unnecessarily bought my book. I extend it to people who want to change jobs and earn more money, but they do not know how to do it, where to start, and most of all, they do not believe that they have a chance to succeed. This guidebook is intended for people with little knowledge of English and those who speak the language quite well. It is also addressed to people looking for work, through which they can achieve a sense of life and financial satisfaction. I want to give you the knowledge on how to look for jobs in various sectors and the correct answer to questions recruiters ask during interviews. Tips contained in the book are based on my experience and the experience of many people I know or I have met during my stay in London.

Phone calls from the university, which I graduated from in the UK in 2008 also contributed to writing this book. The school conducts a yearly survey among former graduates to gather information about how their professional lives changed and what profit they make.

Students of my faculty ring up, asking insightful questions about my start after graduation, job search methods, my current career. They ask for advice, which I gladly impart. From the frequency of calls from the same students I conclude that they like to call me, and that these discussions are very fruitful for them. Unfortunately, I was not able as yet to send them back to my book previously as it was written and published in the Polish language only.

I get numerous phone calls from long-unseen friends who recall me at the time when they want to change jobs, but do not know where to start. They are often people who I used to suggest something, and it worked out good for them. Moreover, those friends who have not benefited from my advice also call me and after three years of being stuck in the same place, they dream of buing a house or apartment, because they have decided to stay here for longer. Often they admit that they fear to ring me up, because they realise that they are stuck in place, while I am over the next stage of career or have bought a new property.

A lot of my projects are a success, therefore, I dare say I am able to direct others as a result of my experience, but I do not consider myself as a super expert and I continue to learn from my mistakes.

I think I have served many people, giving them guidance on the selection of their next job, or how to prepare for the interview, because my interviews mostly ended in success.

Thanks to this, work in banking has become my main source of income and a gateway to a better life.

3
Failure does not make you a loser

What does not kill us, makes us stronger.
Friedrich Nietzsche

Why I did I decide to tell you my story? Because it is true, and you can find it useful. It is possible that you will find in it an impulse to act. I came to London in May 2004. Now I work as a business partner and a financial analyst in banks in the City of London. But the beginnings were not so wonderful as I was not delegated from a Polish bank for a position here (well, I know such lucky ones – do not worry, they are very few). I started from scratch. As all of you are.

Let me slightly elaborate on my story. I want you to be aware of the fact that I am quite an ordinary person, not possessing outstanding capabilities in academic areas, and my English leaves much to be desired. I have gone through a lot in my life, but I did not give in to self-doubt, like a valiant Don Quixote tilting at windmills. If the story, which opens the door to my private life in Poland, does not interest you, please skip to the next chapter.

As a young girl living in Poland initially, I had no notion for my life. Being in my early twenties with two small children and divorced, I did not know how to organise my life. I got a high school diploma and completed a two-year study of computer science. I would add that I was not a honours student in high school, I only benefited from the fact that the school taught English. My confidence was negligible.

Divorce influenced me surprisingly. Until then, I had thought that life would go on a little next to me, it would somehow organise itself without too much of my involvement. Of course, I had different, more or less interesting notions for my life, but they concerned mainly furnishing the apartment (while I was still staying with my husband – then unfortunately we had to sell the flat …), tutoring or knitting. Divorce, however, is an event in life, which can be very encouraging. Having heard from my husband that alone I would surely fail, I woke up in life. A well-known saying: "What does not kill us, makes us stronger" no longer seemed to me such a cliche. I often say it to myself.

Thanks to the determination – here I should thank the Polish system of helping single mothers, who do not have a chance for a normal life, let alone studying at university – each role I undertook, I tried to be a perfectionist, in every way better than others. Only I knew how much it cost me. I worked as a secretary, salesperson of medical supplies (where I met Jacek, my current partner), I ran a small computer shop and I worked as an agent in a bank. All these things happened simultaneously (I already mentioned my two children…). Of course, Jacek took part in all my projects and helped me a lot. Together, we worked on three posts. Not having a higher education, I tried to make up for deficiencies in education and perseverance – I admit – very hard work. At all costs I wanted to prove to myself and others that I could do it!

Many times I had to overcame difficulties to do a project. But I know now the devil is not as black as it is painted, sometimes it is worth it, even in spite of ourselves, to try to put in for a task that seemingly is beyond us, just to stop being afraid and to tame stress. As I have already mentioned, in the company I worked for I met Jacek, my current partner – I was his manager. My hard work paid off after years. He puffed up with pride because of the promotion, but my subordinates (except for Jacek) did not share my enthusiasm, especially because – unlike me – they had university degree. All the time I felt, however, that I lacked self-confidence and self-control.

At some point I realised that I needed to know how to struggle with stress. This applied not only to work – but to private life as well. I got stressed even if I had to sort something out in a bureau (especially revenue). Today, I laugh at this, and I know that everyone has the potential, which they just need to gradually release. I also needed time to wake up a sense of values in me. I realised, too, that it is impossible to completely get rid of stress, but it could be controlled and is usually motivating. Running a small shop cost me a lot of stress. I had been there rarely due to many additional obligations, which I had to cope with, therefore my employee was on his own. At that time, I initiated cooperation with the bank, I was dealing with the sale of commercial loans and acquiring customers, but it was a very stressful job. With such a spate of tasks I worked even on Saturdays. Finally, we were able to buy a car and an apartment on hire purchase. Our jobs engulfed us so deeply that there was no time to talk with children. We gave our best years and hearts to a company we worked for as employees, at the cost of our family.

The decision about going to Dublin (yes, it was our original plan) we made unanimously. We had heard so many fantastic stories about working abroad, we were so hopeful that we decided to take a chance. We were attracted by much higher earnings for normal working hours, better treatment of workers, and above all interesting prospects for children. We decided to leave only the two of us leaving the girls for a year under the care of my mother and grandmother.

4

The conquest of London

He who is not courageous enough to take risks,
they achieve nothing in life.
Muhammad Ali

At the airport in London, we changed our mind. We decided to look around in the capital of the UK. We had the contact addresses of our online friends, therefore, our first steps were directed to them. They welcomed us, probably thinking that in a few days we would go somewhere else. But we decided to stay. For a small fee we rented from them a house in their garden. Basia and her daughter Helena immediately decided to help us. They announced they would seek work for me. In the beginning I was very happy, but my face thinned when Barbara brought the news – I could start in two weeks… housecleaning. I got panicky. As I knew it would soon come to light that I hated cleaning and I did it at home only out of necessity. I broke down. I clung to the idea that, I had learned English and that something of this education remained in my head, so I was hoping to find something more in line with my fantasies. I broke down even more after the first shop at Tesco. I did not understand what an Indian checkout assistant was saying to me. Damn, my English was supposed to be communicative! Well, it was not.

I had two weeks to find another job. Working in a coffee shop was the last resort. I was looking through the local newspapers.

I must admit that I dared to read only the slightest adverts. It occurred to me that in all of them was a phone number and I would have to call to make an appointment for an interview.

In the suitcase I found my resume which I had translated in into English while I was still in Poland. I read it and learned it for two days in order to present myself the best as I could, and specify what I was able to do and what my strengths were.

The fear paralysed me before the interview. I decided to make a few silly phone calls to the numbers in Yellow Pages (car rental, laundry, etc.) just to find out if I could understand the speaker. I called for two days and also went to Tesco. In the end, I made my first phone call about the job. I thought it would have gone worse. Fortunately, the advertiser did not question me, I guess he just did not have time. He accepted applications and made appointments. He explained he was looking for a shop assistant in a gift shop. He only asked me once if I had ever sold anything and where I came from. He gave me the address, that is, he repeated it four times, because I had difficulty putting down everything… you probably guessed I did not even ask about the salary.

I felt faint after the conversation. I felt that it was not supposed to be this way. While in Poland, I had a lot more self-confidence and different idea about my fluency in English. The rest of the day I learned my CV by heart. I said nothing either to Basia or Helena. I knew one thing: at all costs I need to get to the place where I would have contact with native English speakers.

The next day, I went for an interview. I had a long way to go. First, bus trip to Ealing, then the subway red line to Tottenham Court Road, then change to metro black line to Tooting Bec.

Mr Johnson was a black and at first glance, an accessible man. He looked through my CV and unexpectedly said it was not a job for me. I should look for something better, for example, as a salesperson, but in the company, and not in a small shop. I did not expect such a turn of events. I had good qualifications, but I could barely communicate in the target language. After an hour spent on the exchange of arguments (I was a bit slow) I said straight out that, yes, in my country I worked for better positions, but here I would not have such a possibility, until I got more fluent in the language.

I brought my interviewer home to the fact that I had another alternative – housecleaning – and this was not a good way out. Mr Johnson was afraid that I would not pull my weight to such prosaic work. I assured him that thanks to my experience the store could benefit, because I could take care of orders, the visibility of the product and ensure new orders. I asked whether he had at least one such well-qualified person in his shop. I did not think he had, because he laughed and said I could start the following day. He even mentioned, that if I try hard, in half a year I would get the keys to the store.

I was in shock!

It was my first job in London. The rate, a trifle, £4.25 per hour (please remember, it was in 2004). I got home proud of myself. Jacek did not believe that I told him the truth. Only Basia and Helena were disappointed. Well, I would not clean up at their friends'. At least for now.

I guess I had never in my life tried so hard like while working in this store. The shop offered a variety of trinkets from small decorative lamps, figurines, mirrors and pictures to greeting cards. Every day, there was noisy like a beehive. I did not think that so many people bought these things. I received and labelled goods, arranged them on the shelves and, of course, I was serving customers at the counter. I had to admit that the first time at the real one. I spent the whole days with other female employees from different countries, which really helped me to improve my English. I also started to talk more with customers, sometimes even I was able to advise something.

Mr Johnson almost always worked in the shop with us. Perhaps he was familiar with the proverb: "The eye of the master makes the horse fat." After a week, he said he was very happy with me. I was not surprised. In the warehouse all boxes and packaging were arranged by numbers (which was perhaps natural), so finding the product for the customer did not take so long. Also placing a new order took much less time. I rearranged items on the shelves, so that customers did not accidentally drop goods, the more so as the shop was crowded every day. My employer was full of admiration that I commuted from so far away and I was always fifteen minutes before due time. He said, he appreciated it, and often gave me £5 for lunch. You probably have guessed that I put the money by.

Do you think I gave up the implementation of ambitious plans for the future for a while? Nothing could be further from the truth. I used to return home quite late, but every time together with Jacek we listened to CDs of an English phrasebook, mostly I listened, because he fell asleep being so tired (some time ago he started working at a construction site). Listening to phrasebooks from the album, as well as everyday conversations with the girls working in the shop, had a positive impact on my English. I modified my CV and I decided to look for another job. From time to time I had a day off during a week in exchange for work at the weekend. Instead of resting, on days off I sent regularly (we had access to the internet) my CV to companies selling medical supplies, but to no effect. I also brought my resume personally to several dental clinics that were near my place of residence. Also to no avail.

I did not give up. I went for a control visit to one of the clinics in which I submitted my applications. At the reception desk I inquired about the CV I had sent a week before and assured that I was still interested in working there. The receptionist was not very nice, but in general I did not bother about it. As I was passing in the hallway one of the doctors, I accosted him, saying that I left my application at the front desk. It turned out that the doctor was of Polish origin. During the conversation I learned that soon one receptionist was to be dismissed from the clinic.

This bitch did not tell me anything. The doctor intended to reduce day jobs (he was already quite an aging) and was not able to give a pay rise to the current receptionist, so she decided to look for another job. He wanted to take on her place a person who would also work as a dental nurse with patients. He glanced at my CV and promised to call soon. Meanwhile, I continued my work in the gift shop. I got a rise after two weeks and continued trying hard.

One day the doc called.

"Mrs Ada, will you agree to start in a week? I suggest the rate of £7 per hour?"

That was something! "But what shall I say to Mr Johnson!?" In the end, he was very kind to me. A month of my work there passed by, so I decided to simply tell him that I got a better paying job.

I asked him if I could speak to him for a while, and he said that he also had something to say.

"Ms Ada, I'm very pleased to work with you and I'm very satisfied with your work for me. I decided that after a month I will give you the keys to my shop and another pay rise: £5.80 per hour."

What now? How could I say, what I wanted to tell him? I stammered out that I was pleased, but I had unpleasant news. I had to go back to Poland, because my mother felt ill and she could no longer care for children. I came up with this little lie on the spot. I was ashamed as I do not like lying. Mr Johnson was inconsolable.

I started a new job at Doc's. Initially I registered patients for the so the called check-ups and general or root canal treatment. Later, I had to help him in assisting patients. In short, once again I worked at the desk, where I also had the chance to realise in the area of manual tasks. The scope of my duties included the settlement of charges for treatments. Sounds good, huh?

This was immense stress – with every ringing phone! I became aware how different the English accent can be. Sometimes it was impossible to understand who they were and what treatment they wanted to book. I had the greatest difficulty with the Scottish accent and sometimes I was close to tears. But I thought that if I felt uncomfortable to ask someone five times what they mean, in such situations I would say: "Sorry. I cannot hear you, the line is very bad, do you want to book a check-up?" Then, again, I asked the caller to explicitly provide their names.

Fortunately, the doc hardly left his consulting room – probably he would have been very stressed because I did not hear every patient, and probably would have found out it was the fault of the telephone line failure. As a rule, the same patients made appointments at the clinic, therefore over time it got easier because during a conversation over the phone I learned to associate the names. Of course, patients coming to the clinic asked a lot of questions, and although my answers were not perfect, gradually I began to understand what they were saying. Talking on the phone helped me to communicate with people face to face.

I loved this job, especially since I started working in the consulting room with the patients. I prepared and mixed the material for fillings, sterilised instruments in an autoclave, and prepared trays with amenities for patients. Obviously I cleaned up the office. It was not difficult.

Doc came to England with his parents as a boy. Years earlier, he had a much larger clinic, but with age, his needs decreased. The only thing giving him sleepless nights was his daughter, the apple of his eye (of course, attending a private school in London). It seemed to me that he was a nice, honest man. Besides, every Sunday he could be seen at the Mass in the Polish church. However, after some time, I lost heart with him, having heard a couple of times how he estimated the Poles. According to him, they abused the social system, for example by taking child benefits. I will not go into details, but I think that if one pays taxes, they deserve to subsidise the child. It is probably a good thing that parents could buy their child in Poland more things, not to mention the price of separation. Doc would have reported all such people to the police. I, admittedly, did not receive child benefit at that time but I had such an intention, if the state would offer it to me. I took his words to myself.

Doctor grew increasingly interested in my plans for the future. Did he want to make sure how long I would be in the UK to take the air for him and his daughter? Of course, I maintained I wanted to develop my skills and enrol in some courses, who knows, maybe not necessarily as a dental nurse.

For he blurted out: "Ada, how much money are you going to make in the future?"

So I told him "One day I will make £15 per hour"

Doc laughed and asked who would pay so much to a Polish woman and that I would have to settle for wages less than £10 per hour. I thought I would bawl with anger. After all, he also had Polish roots.

And just such moments people need most to find determination in themselves. I decided that I would not stay long in this clinic. Above all, I had to improve my English.

Once the doc went out for lunch, I started to browse the internet in search of the nearest language school. In less than thirty minutes I had a list of five colleges located next to the clinic. After a few phone calls I chose one of them moderately cheap and located quite close by. Classes were held three times a week for two hours in the evenings.

I came to the group in which there were two people from Poland. Our lecturer, although not a native English woman, turned out to be a lovable and very helpful person. There was a huge difference between learning English in high school and learning the language in a real-life environment. I remembered every bit of grammar, but I had a problem with vocabulary. At each meeting we had a quiz. After two months I passed them the best of the whole group – perhaps to spite doc – but I still struggled with fear of speaking in English. I was embarrassed to speak, regardless of the topic. In the school, however, I found out that everyone had their Achilles' heel. One Polish boy spoke excellent English, I envied him. He came to London four years earlier. In school, he studied German, but he did not write in English very well, after all, it was not unusual – he moved in the English environment only. Moreover, he was much younger, at least eight years. He had the advantage over me: the younger a human is, the faster they absorb new language. I had known from the start it would take a lot of time to master to speak the English well. But at least I knew grammar rules well, and that was something.

After four months of studying, my teacher asked me to stay after classes. I was surprised by what she said. She asked why I had not submitted an application for a university so far. She said I continuously improved my writing skills, therefore I would have a good chance to finish school. I could even apply for a grant to study, so-called, student loan. She said that the discussions which sometimes were conducted in the classroom, showed that I had the highest ambitions and that I dreamt of a better life. She noticed that I was looking far into the future. Also, she emphasised that I would have a lot of hard work, because I would have to quickly learn new vocabulary. I promised to think about it. I considered this step as too risky. I had in mind attempts, which I undertook in Poland twice I could not get to the end of the second year of extramural science, because I worked even on weekends. My current teacher told me then that I could at least appear at exams.

And now suddenly I was able to finish university in London? Such a dream…

It was July. In May I would have been staying in the UK for a year. My children had just joined us. And I could not stop thinking about the university and agonised over the thought, how I could reconcile all my responsibilities? At the same time, I would have been working at the clinic for a year. I knew I would get a raise (an additional pound per hour, and that was good, at least I was appreciated). I was happy with the work. On Wednesdays, I would finish work at 2 pm, which was ideal considering the needs of children. I did not know what to do. And then I thought I could ask my employer what he thought about it. In the end, thanks to him I was in Uni.

One day I told him that I was going to go to University. I did not expect he would laugh that much. I was told that

NOWHERE in England would I get accepted as I stood no chance, as opposed to his daughter, who had chosen to study medicine in the future…

In short, the only thing I could do was to select the faculty.

But how would I decide if I had no idea what field of study and what I was suited for. I googled the internet by typing "How to choose a field of study," and I found a lot of different advice, but probably I was intrigued most by SWOT analysis, which, by doing, individuals can easily explore their abilities (for SWOT analysis I allocated in a book a separate chapter, you can take a look at it , there are a few tips). So far I had perceived my occupation in terms of what I had done in Poland, full-time, which was the role of an accountant while running the shop, I prepared a variety of calculations. In the beginning I even did bookkeeping, later I cooperated with an accounting office, because I did not have time for this.

Reflecting on the choice of future career, I considered various contingencies.

In the end I asked myself what was really important to me and what would be important in the future? The answer was prosaic – money. I wished for the children to have a better start than my own, I wanted them to go to a good college and always have support in me, not only mental but financial as well, so my thoughts were focused around a single theme. Which profession would give me most profits after graduation, and quite fast? Because I did admit years were passing by…

In selecting the field of study, newspapers helped me a lot. I looked through all, one by one, checking out earnings. And it was the best thing I had ever done. Management Accountant – £48,000 a year. Earning even half of that – it would be something! I looked through many other newspapers and each time just this profession seemed to me as the best paid one, with earnings from £45,000 to £60,000 a year. In fine print it was written ACCA Qualified. Whatever it meant, I immediately browsed the Internet, searching for a university that offers a specialisation in accounting. I found five of them, the two included the information that they provided to ACCA certification.

I checked what it meant. These institutions had collaborated with the ACCA association, which respected the exams passed at those universities as eligible for roles reserved for qualified specialists – analysts and accountants. Of course, the deadline for submitting applications had passed a long time before, but there was held so called clearing – some fields still continued recruitment. I had to write an application and submit it together with a CV and a certificate attesting success in the IELTS exam, which unfortunately I did not have. But I was so determined that, after all, I submitted an application to university. The teacher from the college showed me on the internet addresses of the institutions to which I could apply for a student loan to pay for education. I realised that I would not be able to study in absentia, work with doc and look after the children. Having discussed it with Jacek I decided for full-time studies. This meant abandoning work at doc's. All charges and liabilities would have to be covered by Jacek.

Doc balked when I told him three universities responded to my applications and I could start from October. I told him that I was going to give up work at the end of September.

He asked only to recommend him someone to take over my role. I did not know anyone who could replace me, but after a while a Polish girl looking for work in London called to the clinic. In Poland, she worked as a dental nurse in Gdynia and she was going to London in search of her boyfriend. I did not know her, but I decided to be useful and said that she had good timing, because I was just leaving in two weeks. I remember how very happy she was. She could not believe that just after arrival she would have a job interview, and it was going to be at the clinic.

My family in Poland unfortunately did not support my choice. I tried twice to do a university course in Poland, always ending in the second year. Also, my friends were not able to understand how I could quit such a good job in favour of study, which I probably would not manage to finish. After all, "What good a Ferrari is, without a steering wheel", and I wanted to give it up. At first I was angry, then I was sorry, and in the end I asked myself "What am I doing, damn it?!" I have dependent children, and I intend to pursue my dreams. "Could it all right?" I felt that Jacek also had doubts, but he always stood by me, so now he did not question my decision either.

And so I ended one phase of my life in the United Kingdom.

5
Studies and career step by step

The man has in life either excuses or results.
Jack Canfield

Then the day of recruitment came. I was afraid of this moment very much, because I did not hold any certificate attesting fluency in the English language. When submitting documents in the secretarial office, I tried to speak correctly, emphasising that I had been working in the UK for some time and did not think that such a certificate might be I needed.

I got away with that. They just included an info in my documentation, that if necessary, I would deliver a certificate at a later date. Phew, I was able to handle that, it made my day, I became a student of the first year of the Accounting & Finance. I was waiting for confirmation of my student loan.

The first year was more to me than very difficult. I did not understand most of the lectures, I had to take a lot of notes to explain dozens of words. I am not going to hide back that I stayed up till four in the morning studying. In Uni I had very complex subjects. I could not imagine how I would deal with exams. Somehow, I could manage with writing essays by spending hours in the library and bringing home tons of books. Even my daughters were disturbed. They were then twelve and thirteen years old and they would never imagine they would see their mum hitting the books at night. It was for them really inspiring and motivating.

And I had doubts whether I did right, giving up the work and deciding to study. Sometimes I felt that I would not be able to get through three years of university, even though I promised myself that I would do everything in my power to persevere, the more that my English gradually improved. In the second term we would write essays in groups of five, so I had to intensively communicate in the target language. Gradually I gained authority among colleagues, because I appeared at the classes the best prepared of the whole group, usually with a lot of materials. Well, everyone wanted to be with me in one team.

I did not have to retake any of the exams. I could not believe that. The first year was over. Of course, I will not wind you up that I scored 100%, but I received a pretty good average final result.

The second year of study, I started full of energy and faith that I could move mountains. There had been a lot of new subjects and again I hit the books at night. The children looked at me with growing admiration. All of a sudden, in the middle of the year just before exams, I began to feel an incredible fatigue and I was losing faith in the meaning of what I was doing. As you can see, I had the moments of doubt. I was terrified because I was approaching the halfway point of study, and I was aware that I could not take in any more information. As if I had run out of my capacity for knowledge. As if I could not go any further. I was tired, I cried.

My elder daughter approached me and tried to comfort me. She told me what I was always telling her.

"Mum, first you say that nothing is impossible, and since childhood you have been pushing me to study medicine, even though I cannot understand biology and chemistry, and now you sit here and do not study for exams. I can just say that you give up. After all, you said that you would have such a cool job after the graduation."

Actually. Yes, I said so. I bent my both daughters' ears that they would have to be accepted to medicine or dentistry. Period! They would have to have a profession that would give them the money, satisfaction and confidence that they would always find a job. What was now happening to me? But if I did not pass a test on the first approach, I could retake it. I would re-sit as many exams as I would manage. Most people from my year re-took exams two or three times. I had not failed even one as yet. But I would not have to be perfect.

My younger daughter (a terrible tyke and keen to tease) also tried to cheer me up, saying:

"Oh, mummy, mummy, you are just pretending, and then you will still get Straight A's. You can do it!"

I got a grip, because I had only a week, and four more exams, fortunately three concerned counting and only one theory.

As you probably guessed it, I did not get enough sleep the night before the exams. I passed all four – I passed two of them earning a minimum number of points, but still enough to apply for ACCA certification. I felt relieved. Upon returning home after the last exam I just passed out. Nobody dared to wake me up, I was well away.

The second term passed without any major problems. In March, I decided to look for a part-time job. I had fewer classes, because I gave up on lectures but I focused on seminars. In addition, I decided that it would be good to find a job worthy of an ambitious CV, which would indicate that already in Uni, I was active in the work market.

I edited my CV. I focused on the experience gained in Poland and subjects that I studied at university. I realised that with the experience of a professional dental nurse or receptionist I would not find adequate employment for the field of my study. I began to send my CV to the agencies which I found on the internet. The two agencies responded that they wanted to meet me. And indeed, after the first call I received a job offer – to do a translation of a short interview with one of our Polish weightlifters. It was paid £7.20 per hour. Good to start with. Later I was receiving from the agency other offers of quite simple translations. But I decided not to include this experience in my CV.

The other agency, however, came in handy the most. On exactly my thirty-third birthday I got a phone call that they needed a person for the position of an assistant to a Company Secretary for a period of three, or four months, three times a week for £12 per hour. Mind you, I did not even have to complete studies to earn more than £10 per hour. I wanted to call doc.

The company was a well-known one, bringing together the main attractions in London. They obviously sought someone with at least three years' experience (at that time, not knowing what kind of position it might be, I was wondering why the assistant to a secretary needed three years' experience and why they paid so well), but they needed someone immediately, I was invited for an interview.

It turned out that the person I would be replacing was ill and would be on a sick leave for quite a long time. A Company Secretary is a very high position in the hierarchy, just after the boss. The new boss also explained me that my predecessor earned £50,000 a year. I must admit that my jaw dropped. I realised that I still had a lot to learn. My future boss also said that she rarely happened to be present in the office, and that in a couple of weeks she was going on a vacation, hence they needed to employ someone immediately.

The work was not very difficult, but my deficiency in English pestered me. Also, the rest of the team was not favourable to me (please remember, it was 2006). Initially I was responsible for organising legal documents, watching deadlines, monitoring fleet of company cars, running spreadsheets to calculate different fees. So, everything I had no idea how to deal with. Things got even more complicated after three weeks when my boss went on vacation, leaving me a brief note on paper and an email that I would need to register new companies on a special website.

She wanted me to begin to fill in forms online and then sent them online, as draft documents – on her return corrected registrations were to be sent again. The idea was to reserve the registration deadline, because it was quite urgent. She gave me only the first letters of the names of companies, each consisting of three or four words. I received six different abbreviations (eg .: MTAL, ATLE). I had never registered companies, and the thing is they were to be registered within the same organisation as its subsidiaries (another London Attractions) made it all even more complicated. So I began my quest for information. How to find out what the full names of companies were? Finally, I managed to reach out to one of the managers who responded to my email, stating the full names of the newly created subsidiaries. That was something. I found the forms and began to fill them in. It turned out, however, that I could not save them in the internet on a website of that institution. I found the required phone number and I was able to get through to a very nice person who said that a new system had just been introduced recently and forms could not be filled in and then corrected online. In order to the registration took place in time, I would have to fill in all the forms once and submit them immediately. Unfortunately, the adjustment would be possible only after a year.

Despite the enormous stress I decided to fill in the documents myself. I thought that because I was with this challenge alone, I would gain an opportunity to show initiative and beat the damn stress. I was able to find in the archives two old forms, and the person I spoke to was very helpful. She checked the previous forms which were filed in a year or two years ago and gave me the relevant information.

In fact, thanks to her, I was able to fill all the documents and send them as expected by my supervisor. I was dying of fear. When my boss returned, I did not get in her way, until I was asked if the registration forms had been sent and whether we could get copies to include corrections. You should have seen her face when I told her that the forms, indeed, had been sent, but the system had been changed and they no longer could be corrected online. She froze. My hands were shaking as I handed her the copies. She checked them and said with relief that the documents had been completed properly. She also said that she had made the right choice by hiring me, even though my English left much to be desired, and the experience was negligible. She said that the Poles were intelligent people. Ha, ha, very nice.

After four months, I finished my work on the contract in the Attractions. Of course, at once I updated my CV.

The third year at university was very busy. I had to decide what faculty I would ultimately choose. Taxation or Management Accounting? Of course, I chose Management Accounting, because I never wanted to have my own accounting office, I was not going to take care of filling tax returns either. Again, I attended seminars only, as all days I studied for exams. Examinations of the first and second term I passed with good results. I graduated with the title of Bachelor.

Everyone breathed with a sigh of relief.

6
The winning streak in London

*Patience and perseverance have a magical effect -
thanks to them difficulties disappear and obstacles evaporate.*
John Quincy Adams

Shortly after exams I sent my CV to recruitment agencies. I was not sure how long I would look to find a new job. In response to my application, the same agency, through which I received a job while studying, came back to me. My consultant said I got very good references from Attractions, and invited me for an interview. Probably he would have the next role for me. But I promised myself that when I finished University, I would take a long vacation and would rest! None of this. A new job was waiting for me.

The agency openly communicated to me that in response to the job advertisement they put two other candidates for the interview. I was afraid of rejection immensely. I was the only one who did not have the UK citizenship. The company's management, however, accepted my resume and wanted to see me. I prepared to the interview very carefully. I had to be better than the British candidates. I studied my CV, emphasising my strengths and abilities. In this respect, I analysed both my professional experience with the period of work in Poland and competence gained in London. I tried to match my professional experience and personal features to the job description which I applied for. Unfortunately, except for one part-time job in England I had not anything more to boast about as yet.

I wanted to look professional, so I invested in a grey jacket and skirt set. I checked the website of the organisation in which I tried to get a job with great attention. The company dealt with the marketing, specialising in advertising campaigns. At the interview, I met my future manager, a ginger-haired , very energetic and confident woman. In the company she held the position of a Financial Controller. The role, which I had applied for was a Purchase Ledger Clerk. The person who would be hired for this position would be responsible for the introduction of invoices, payments, settlement of accounts, accounting transaction. The recruiter asked me a lot of questions, including how I coped with stress, what I could bring to the team and why the company should hire exactly me. As soon as I left the meeting, I felt a huge relief, but also dissatisfaction. I thought that I could do more to advertise and highlight my advantages. And… my English – I used a couple of times Polish expressions. Well, it was my first major interview, so there was no reason to fall apart, "The first pancake is always spoiled."

I was very surprised when the agency worker rang up with the news that I was invited for the second interview, this time with the director. I shivered at the thought that once again I would have a huge stress and learning by heart all these interview questions. The director was quite curt, the interview was short, and questions similar to the previous ones. Now, all I could do was wait. After a week I received the information from the agency that I was accepted. This was beyond my wildest expectations. Again, I got the job after the first interview! The agency told me that my candidacy was most insisted on by the ginger-haired woman. The director had objections. I guessed it was about my terrible English. I was offered a salary of £22,500 a year plus a private retirement and health insurance. I should have now gone to the doc and SHOUT IT OUT!

I must confess that I started to stress at that moment. I could not sleep from nerves before my first day of work. I did not know what awaited me, if someone would put me through what computer program the company used and, above all, whether people in the team would like me and if they would be helpful. It turned out that they were all very nice and I learned a lot there. Only my boss was a ghost and did not allow us to live. But I clenched my teeth and I used the expertise of people who had several years of experience. Everyone was afraid of the boss, but after a while they began to say that I had beneficent influence on her. I was always nice, smiling and willing to work, helping others when I had a free moment, and thus I learned new things. Btw, my English got better and better.

After ten months, I received a promotion to the position of Accounts Assistant, with income rate of £23,500 a year. I got a new task: I was responsible for marketing agreements settlements. During a conversation in private I learned from the ginger-haired woman that she was very satisfied with my work and that she knew from the beginning that my engagement would be a good choice.

But I was slowly beginning to have enough of this. The atmosphere in the company was not very nice and after a few months I decided that I wanted to look for another job. Again, I sent out my CV to recruitment agencies. This time, a few of them were interested in meeting me. I attended all the interviews. After talking with recruiters, I decided that I wanted to look for work on the contract, not permanent. It turned out that with such an agreement hourly rate was higher. I decided to give notice of cancellation in such time, so I could say goodbye to the company just before Christmas. I had a month's notice period. My boss was very upset because her assistant was also about to leave her job, and therefore I was going to be offered another promotion, this time to the position of Assistant Financial Controller. Well, apparently it was not my destiny. I did not regret this, however. I was glad that I did not have to work for two or three months during the notice period, and such conditions are the norm after two years of employment, depending on the contract.

I spent Christmas holidays in Poland in pleasant atmosphere without thinking about work at all. I was glad that I was able to persevere in the company for a year and a half, and my CV appreciated in value. Having returned I called various agencies constantly, finding out about available jobs. In the end, I was sent to two interviews. I did not get the first job, but the interview proved to be a good workout before the next one, because during the meeting I was given the third degree.

The other interview went much better. Finally, I already knew my CV by heart, and on the internet I retraced most questions which could appear at an interview. The next day I got a reply that they wanted to offer me a job and £14.50 per hour, a contract for four months and the post of an Assistant Financial Controller. That was the rate, which I could not believe, all the more as my CV was not impressive at all yet. Now I knew that the secret lies in the technique of interview and not in perfect English and vast experience.

The company was of average size and dealt with investing in the stock market in various sectors. It belonged to three brothers who really cared about their employees. Once a week, each of us had allocated half-hour back massage performed by a specialist, and lunch to choose from a variety of gourmet teas and coffees, delicious cakes and other sweets, not to mention the fruit. I saw also how much people who trade at the stock market differ from others. They were talking to themselves all the time, walking back and forth around the office, vividly gesticulating, etc. Sometimes you might get scared, but mostly it was just fun. These individuals were selected from among the best students of Oxford and Cambridge.

The work turned out to be not stressful and I was often able to deal with all the tasks ahead of time. I was responsible for implementing processes such as Trial Balance, Cash Flow, P & L Reconciliation, Fixed Assets Register and other calculations. The company was located on High Street Kensington, so I had the opportunity to eat lunch in a relaxed atmosphere and charming scenery.

7

If you want to live in life – become a banker

If you want to live after death – become an artist,
if you want to live in life – become a banker.
Andrzej Majewski

When the contract in the bank was coming to an end, again I sent out my CV, supplemented by further positions and professional experience. This time I received a lot of phone calls. They offered me a different rate from £10 to £14 per hour. Consistently, I turned down all the proposals to work for a rate below £14. Not only that, after reviewing the websites of prestigious recruitment agencies I noticed that working in banks, especially on contracts, was much better paid. In addition, senior specialists received daily rates, which equalled my weekly wage. I could not believe my eyes when I realised that I could earn so much. Unsurpassed dreams. But the appetite grew with eating. And very well. Each agency which was contacting me was informed that I wanted to work in a bank and I was waiting for jobs that meet my expectations. In response, I heard that I had not worked in a bank and had no chance of getting such work. The circle is closed. If no one I could offer me work in the bank, how shall I get it? I had to admit that I was disappointed and angry. After all, it was illogical. At that point even the rate did not matter to me, I only wanted to work in a bank.

Then suddenly someone called from an agency with the information that they could have something interesting for me, on condition I would have to decide to transfer. In such moments you need to show flexibility, because the end justifies the means. I replied that, yes, I was able to do this for a dream job and for a lot of money. I was offered a job on the island of Jersey, in the XXX bank. I needed a few seconds to decide. Yes, please send my CV! In the end, it was not said that they would accept me, but it was worth giving a try. I did not even try to imagine how I would convey this news to my family.

The agency informed me the bank needed someone immediately. People with vast experience have no problem finding a job in London, they do not have to move in pursuit of work, besides they usually have families, so this moving out for them is unrealistic. The next day, the agent informed me that the bank was interested in my application. I had an appointment for a telephone conference call, involving two persons representing the XXX bank. Well, that I did not predict. Interview over the phone – probably there was nothing worse. Again, I looked through all the questions and answers and specifications of the offered position. Then came the day. I had such a headache that I was thinking that I would go crazy. Why did I need so much stress?! I had better pursue the goal in small steps. Maybe in the end I would find work in the bank somewhere in London? After all, why did I reject offers of less than £14 per hour? Gaining experience is also important, not only gaining a lot of money.

In the end, the interview took place. Audibility was not the worst, I had to use my famous question: "The line is very bad, can you come again, please?" only once. After the conference, I prayed to God that the bankers would contact me as soon as possible. They did. And they had good news for me at the weekend. I was over the moon.

I did not think children would be so pleased with my success. Jacek said he would try to come back from work earlier – someone would eventually have to make lunch for the children and ensure their school homework was done. He surprised me very positively. Immediately everyone started to study the map of Jersey and watch the pictures of local beaches. The island is famous for its wonderful views and tranquillity, and therefore is called the island of retirees. Staying on it is quite expensive, the food fantastic, and the beaches are not populated at all. It is usually warmer than in the UK.

We established an action plan. Jacek had to reorganise his plan of the day and the children were given one list of things that would have to be done, and the other list of things that were absolutely forbidden. Just in case, because I still remembered as two years before they were baking fries in the oven – although in my presence, but I was not supposed to interfere, because they were already 'adults'. Suddenly I heard a cry "Fire!". When I ran into the kitchen, my two daughters passed me, running in the opposite direction. It turned out that fire was raging in the oven. Having put out the fire, I left the kitchen in search of the children. One of the daughters was wrapped in a blanket in her bed, so tightly that I could not unwrap the blanket from her and the other one with the rabbit under her arm, was standing ready to evacuate at the entrance door which were wide opened. I would like to add that the rabbit is our pet. And under the arm of my daughter should be her younger sister. Therefore, it was necessary to establish certain safety rules.

But back to the topic, the most important was school, especially the girls were preparing for GCSEs. This aspect aroused my greatest doubts in terms of the departure. The daughters had to take exams on twelve subjects, including obligatory Chemistry, Physics and Biology. This choice, of course, was my idea, because I felt guilty that I would not be there so that I could help them.

The work started a week before May long weekend. Still, I could not believe it. Such cash! And in addition, in a bank. A dream come true. The flight lasted thirty-five minutes. I was intoxicated by beautiful landscapes and wonderful sea air. The road from the airport led mostly along the coastline. I fell in love with the island at first sight. Even nowadays, we go there on weekends and holidays. Jersey is my second home.

The team who I worked with proved to be very sympathetic. They were mostly young people who did not mind leaving London. They marvelled that I decided to stay away from home and family for five months. I was shown the apartment. It was small, but most charming. It was on the High Street full of chain stores, which offered huge discounts and prices without VAT. In a nutshell, a shopping paradise. I immediately got into organising the arrival of my family for the long weekend. Unfortunately, it turned out that they could not sleep in my apartment. It was a studio, and in addition business one. Only two people could stay in it. And, here I met a nice surprise. The head of the bank suggested that he would pay for the hotel, if my loved ones came over. Just no one took into account the fact that I had a family. I was left speechless. It really was a very nice gesture. The weekend was fantastic. My girls were enchanted with the island, Jacek and I with amazing food. All treats fresh straight from the sea! Even the weather was fine for us.

But following the main thread. As a Management Accountant I was responsible for preparing spreadsheets, which I loaded into the system and the various reports of cost. I also started to participate in the process Budgeting & Forecasting. For the first time also I carried out MI Reporting. I had to admit that the tasks awaiting me seemed to me to be quite complicated, but the person that I would have to replace, really conscientiously explained me my duties, and for sure I prepared a lot of notes. Everything was new to me and difficult, especially since I missed terribly my close ones. In spite of everyday conversations on Skype, I shed tears. It was the hardest time for me. Every other weekend I flew back home. It was difficult for me, especially when I did not understand anything at work and I was afraid to ask four times about the same thing. I had no one to get it all off my chest. Every day I was alone. I tried to go out with my team after work to speak in English, but I could not enjoy these meetings. Lonely walks on the beach did not soothed my homesickness.

Finally, five months were over. I was incredibly glad that soon I would be back to London! My CV gained splendour and landed in all possible recruitment agencies. No wonder that very soon there was a response. Many agencies offered me a job in London with a package of attractive financial conditions, where rates were similar to earnings, which I received in the XXX bank, or even higher. It was amazing how many doors to the banks in London were opened by the work in a bank on the island. This gave me confidence and I felt much more comfortable in dealing with employment agencies. When I talked about a specific post, I could negotiate and ask difficult questions. I no longer had to phone the agency day by day. Now, they courted my interest. They scented a good deal, because as a former bank employee I received, not an exorbitant rate for a particular industry, and therefore agencies, by commending me to their clients, counted on making much profit on me. Before I left the island, I had appointments for three interviews with three different agencies. Needless to say, that each of them offered me a job in a bank, and with the daily rate! I could not believe that I had a chance to earn so much money. I tried to approach this from a distance, but I had to admit that I felt a sought-after.

After returning from Jersey l was lazing about all day, and the next day I was hard at work.

I had to learn to talk convincingly about my last, banking job vacancy. I was looking through the internet in search of new questions and answers for the interview. It annoyed me that there was no single website where all possible questions and answers could be gathered, and of course in English. It would facilitate immensely my preparations. But do not worry, I'm thinking about creating the site where interested individuals will be able to benefit from a complete list of questions and appropriate answers used in recruitment process. Look for www.career-24.co.uk in the future.

The first interview (with the employees of the bank offering to work with a rate of £100 a day!) did not go well. I was put off by my interlocutor. I was questioned by two people: the man was very nice, but when it turned out that he would not be my boss, I lost my enthusiasm. The woman was curt, she spoke only about obligations, observance of working hours and stress. After thirty minutes, I knew that I would not get the job. And so it happened. But I have never regretted that.

The second interview (the rate of £180 to £220 a day) rolled over in my thoughts. I was offered the position, but due to lack of experience in the banking industry I was offered the lower rate of £180 a day.

Of course, I was very happy. In general, I was not expecting that at the start I would get

a better deal than in Jersey. Driven by greed, I decided to wait till the third interview.

The girl who advertised me to the bank was very resolute and I think that very streetwise. She immediately said that we would try to win quite good money. She did not say how much. She asked me to do my best. So far, the bank was happy with all of its candidates.

The work was attractive, therefore I studied my CV and questions for a very long time.

The interview was not easy. I was asked a lot of questions about teamwork and stress,

and questions concerning jurisdiction. I was well prepared. I replied profoundly to all the issues raised. I was waiting for a long time for the answer. The agency staff informed me that they just had a few other candidates. I broke down a little, because I had already clinched the job for £180 a day and I did not know how long I could delay to reply them.

In the end, I received a call from the agency with the information that I got the job. With joy I forgot I did not know daily rate yet. The agent gave me a great surprise. The rate, which she negotiated for me, amounted to £275 a day! I thought I was dreaming. I was so excited I did not understand what she said to me. After all, it is money, which I did not even dreamed of, because it was not at all realistic. You guessed it, I received a great position – Assistant Business Partner, with a contract for six months.

My main task was to exercise financial control over costs, the calculation of risk and monthly MI Reporting. In addition, I was entrusted with control over eighty-six projects, the care of the budget, reporting financial performance among different divisions. I worked on a very responsible position. Every day I had a lot of responsibilities and a lot of deadlines. The first two months were the worst, after that everything went smoothly. I was glad that I gained new experience, also participated in the meetings, which for me was a challenge. All the time I lacked confidence. What is true I had no longer problems in composing emails, but speaking English was still very stressful for me, especially in the larger group. Well, one could not have everything. When my contract was ending, I was very tired. I felt that everything happened too quickly.

Financial progress also meant more responsible positions, and that I would have to learn very quickly. Maybe, I should look for a permanent job and spend a year or two in one place, to be able to learn and master thoroughly some aspects of banking? I realised, however, that I did not have time, and if there was such a possibility, then I needed to use it, here and now. The more my enthusiasm reached its zenith, and the lack of knowledge caught up with hard work, often after hours. To work for less money, I could always return when winning streak would be over. There is a proverb: "One might as well be hanged for a sheep as for a lamb."

Another half a year was gone. It was time to refresh my resume and go job hunting.

And again, I used the same pattern: send out CV to agencies, a few phone calls, the intensive preparations for interviews.

As usual, my CV was sent to several positions for different banks. Four agencies called me back, I was not picky, I dreamed that I would be offered, at least such a rate as I received in my previous work. The first meeting unfortunately I failed, the second one in turn went well. After a week they were supposed to speak to me again, but I was afraid that in the end they would find someone with knowledge of the Khalix program, because these were the prerequisites. Here they offered £265 a day. I did not get this work either.

The third interview I considered to have been very successful. They sought people with knowledge of the Polish language because of the duty of controlling the costs of the vehicle fleet in the Polish branch. Unfortunately, the position was not very interesting, but the financial conditions aroused my enthusiasm: £300 as the daily rate and the ability to work at home, for example, once a week. It was tempting. Especially the pay. I came back home and I began to wonder if I would ever hear back from the agency.

It is amazing how suddenly everything could change. On the same day, just before 10 pm, late in the evening, the phone rang, it was someone from the agency. It was quite strange. As far as I know, agents are used to working late, to be able to meet the expectations of their demanding customers. However, to phone so late was a bit suspicious. The agent found my resume on a website. He offered me the position of Division Support Business Analyst, which had quite wide range of salary: £350 to £450 Pounds a day, depending on the experience of the candidate. He liked my CV. During the interview he offered to submit my candidacy at the rate of £400 a day. If my financial expectations would prove to be too high in relation to my skills, which would be verified during the interview, they could always offer me less money.

Initially, I was stressed out, but finally I decided that I had nothing to lose, besides I did not really believe that this late phone would bring any real results. I agreed that the agent forwarded my CV, and that was it. Still, I could not sleep or eat. I was waiting for a message. They called on the next day. I could come for the interview. Then the phone rang again – about the third interview. And here I was offered the job! For the already mentioned £300 per day. The man from the agency complimented on the offer and on my person, ensuring that during the interview I presented myself great and clients were very satisfied.

Of course, a normal and down to earth person would accept the job with a smile like a melon slice on their face and would not dream about £400 per day. In spite of all common sense and folk proverbs such as: "a bird in hand..." I replied that unfortunately I could not answer, because I was having another interview the following day for much better value for money and more interesting position. The agent was stunned and ceased to be nice to me. He asked only what my chances of getting a job for such a rate was if my most recent earnings were £275 a day ("Could he have seen with doc?") I admitted I stood little chance, but I was willing to try. I asked him directly what he would do if he were me. I heard silence. At the end he said that the client would not wait, and in the handset I heard an angrily spoken: "Goodbye."

Then I just got scared. To my mind came passages from *The Wedding* by Polish writer Stanislaw Wyspianski: "You boor, had a golden horn, you boor, had a hat with a feather..."

I was sure that in a normal situation I would have never remembered this quote. I was scared that my greed would lead to my fall. Well, those who do not risk, they do not drink champagne!!!

Soon I was invited by the agent of the evening phone call for the second interview, this time with the director of the bank. It took my breath away. It went well, I was moving forward. But did not believe what would happen. Shortly before the second interview the former agent called me, the one who negotiated my contract for employment for £300 a day. He asked, how my interview was. I replied that it went well and that I was going to have another one. And he told me that the client wanted to wait for me and if I could let him know right away, as soon as I made a decision. Why was I not surprised? I would add that once again he was nice to me. But, I admit that it took a weight off my mind. It was an ideal situation. One job for good money had already been clinched, I was not so stressed out with the second interview. I was just waiting for the fight for my dream position. The first time I went for an interview I was a little laid-back. The meeting lasted maybe thirty minutes. I was eagerly waiting for feedback. In the end, I received the message. And it seems to me that the man from the agency, who negotiated the job for me for £300, perhaps would feel offended for a longer period. I got my dream job. They did not even negotiate rates – £400 a day. God, I used to dream to earn as much in a week. I love London! This city is full of miracles, which must be earned. Oh, I will work very hard!

I signed a contract for five months. The bank was not located in the centre of London, so I had better access to the company. Frankly, it was pretty hard work, but not so stressful, people were very nice. I was assigned a wide range of duties, from preparing spreadsheets, preparing analyses and filling out forms, to the budget, the P & L Accounts and testing models. I was also responsible for the analysis of customer migration between regions and, as usual the MI Reporting, which consisted of costs and revenues and analysing products. Due to the high amount they paid me, every day I was afraid that supervisors would give me a task which would exceed my competence, and I would not be able to handle this, but fortunately new tasks, although I had many of them, were not bothersome. There were also easy and they differed from what I had done before. However, the pace of work did not make me dizzy, so I could slowly deploy and learn. I approached the work in this bank as a reward for the gruelling battle which I fought in the previous bank. I venture to say that I rested a little – well, before the next fight.

And by the way – I was on cloud nine, and I was very proud of myself. The family did not know what was going on. My relatives were aware that I would definitely trudge ahead, but they did not expect that at this rate. It was really motivating for them. I was glad that, especially my children, did not see me stifled by the hard work for miserable money. From the autopsy they learned that the best thing a human could do was to invest in themselves, and then to believe that they could fulfil this dream, if only they followed previously designated paths.

And so another five months passed by. I decided to take advantage of the fact that I was liked not only by colleagues, but also by the head of my department. I asked him about the possibility of cooperation with another team. After two days, he informed me that in the bank in central London there was a vacant post, and he once worked with the local manager. He checked my daily rate and told me that they were recruiting for the position of Finance Manager and I should demand a higher rate, for example, £450, the extra was due to the fact that I would work on Liverpool Street. I was afraid that my expectations were perceived as too high. However, I listened to his advice and sent my resume to his manager. I was invited for an interview and then waited for the response.

A recruitment agency mediated in negotiations. I was offered the same rate that I had before. Common sense would dictate accepting this proposal without questioning, but as appetite grows with eating, I turned to the agency with the information that I hoped for a raise. My ex-boss helped me immensely. He called the lady manager and talked with her, exposing me solid references. Even though my conditions were not accepted, I did not change my mind. I knew that I had to start looking for work in other recruitment agencies.

I admit that afterwards I began to regret my persistence. I kicked myself that my greed lost me. But a man learns all their life. A life likes to surprise. After a week, the bank once again contacted me, offering me the rate... £450! I was speechless. After all, I was not fully qualified! Banks always check the candidates in terms of criminal record and solvency, which is a possible bankruptcy. And I had still actual check and the bank did not have to repeat in detail all the verification procedure. It usually takes two to three weeks. If since the last job two weeks had passed, they needed to carry out a detailed verification.

And so once again I landed in the City, in a very large department. I was responsible for most of the consolidation Board Pack for different departments. I took part in the creation of the budget and the restructuring of the financial department, moreover, I was responsible for product analysis. In short, I had a lot of work after hours, but weekends I spent shopping, of course reasonably, because already during the previous contract I began to look for a house. I was looking for something outside of London. Together with Jacek we placed on a deposit. I wanted to buy a bit of a larger property, but my employment history only allowed to buy a terraced house, but at least in newly built housing estate. Three bedrooms plus a study room, a not very large kitchen plus a small living room. I was not fussy. Unfortunately, by doing this, I extended the time of commuting to London, but it was worth it. I could live in a wonderful area, with a panoramic view of the forest through the windows, in all four corners. We were able to pay 20% of the value of our property. My hard work brought results. I immediately forgot about the whole stress and drudgery combined with work. My own house made up for everything.

When the contract came to an end, I tried to find a new job as soon as possible. I had yet to furnish our house. Since I already settled in the banking industry and I knew more people in this environment, I sent several emails to friends asking for a vacancy. It turned out that one of the senior managers, Mr B., who worked with us in the team, was going to move to a new project to another bank's headquarters, one Tube stop away. He offered to ask around, because he got to know me a little and he would willingly support me.

After a week I had an appointment to speak with the local director, but Mr B. appeared at the meeting. The interview was agreed in the coffee shop and it seemed that almost all the questions of my potential boss were first answered by Mr B. He was well versed what my previous responsibilities were. Since Mr B. exhaustively answered almost all the questions of the director recruiting me, I briefly told about my previous positions and experience. The director immediately informed me that I was accepted. After verifying my application by the agency, I undertook a new job. Probably you guessed that this time I was not going to negotiate rates. I prayed that it would not be lowered. Fortunately, everything was fine.

Formally, I served as Business Analyst, although after a few weeks, I came to the conclusion that due to the tasks performed I rather work as Finance Analyst. I signed a contract for six months, but it seemed to be for a long cooperation. It was a very difficult period. The bank was then in its phase of creating a separate unit. Our department appeared on the front pages of newspapers. I co-created the history of London's financial world. That was something! I was responsible for the MI Board Pack, which I had to create from scratch. I was doing a variety of complex analysis and compilation. We were exposed to the constant changes which were the results of the restructuring of the department. My contract was extended three more times. It gave me a chance to apply for another loan.

Some time before I set my sights on a detached house with five bedrooms, bordered on one side only with the adjacent landscaped grounds. I was enchanted by a beautiful garden, surrounded by a row of rhododendrons which spread along. They bloomed in purple. I was impressed with the old majestic oaks growing around – landscapes recalling a Polish enclave. With my mind's eye I saw myself in a beautiful natural setting, sitting by the fire (well, barbecue is not the same) and absorbing the blissful tranquillity reigning there. I mobilised Jacek to put aside funds for the next deposit. He had no other choice. He also really liked the plot, especially the garden, which for London was huge. And so, thanks to this contract I fulfilled another dream. The bank verified the request for another very long loan. In the end I got it. I had to declare that I would rent the previously purchased house, so as not to expose ourselves to the risk of insolvency as a result of the repayment of the two loans.

It worked, I earned my El Dorado. I ordered a large wooden table (and four chairs) as we moved in the day before Easter. This time we did not go to Poland, but it was one of the best holidays we had ever spent in England. After a month I bought a cubic meter of firewood and a large outdoor fireplace. I was in the seventh heaven.

The work was hard, but returns home, though long, rewarded me everything. The contract lasted one year and seven months, so far it was my longest cooperation with the bank under a single contract. Immediately after its expiry, I managed to slip on to the next chapter, in the same bank. The agency had in this matter little to do. In practice, I would find new roles myself. Agents were settling only formalities. This time I also decided to find another contract myself by reviewing my notebook with contacts. I needed this job to build up my resources after buying the second house. After a few days I had my next job.

I signed a contract for five months. A new department was just being created, and I was responsible for building the structure and supervision that accompanied the changes. On my head were other challenges: cost control and financial risk, cuts under the new budget, reports generation, and of course, Flash and Board Pack. Working in a small team, occupying a fairly high position in the hierarchy of the organisation proved to be rather quiet. Other units were subjected to us, which reported to us. Pretty good position at the end of work in the YYY bank.

But I must admit that I felt tired. I had no holidays, no free time for myself, I did not have time to rest, and the years were passing by. After the expiration of the contract I decided to just stay in my beloved home and indulge in sweet doing nothing. In the end, I deserved a reward for 1000% normal schedule!

So as I promised, I savoured now staying at home, but instead of lazing around, I started to write a book. I still get a lot of phone calls from friends - those close and distant ones.

I serve them with help and advice, regardless of the situation. Sometimes I help someone to prepare for the interview, I browse the internet, come across new agencies and interview questions. I do CV checks, sometimes I edit them and I adapt to a specific job. It happens that I mediate between the agency and the candidate or issue a reference to people who deserve to support their own work and determination in building their career. I have a lot of cool ideas, often I impart a fairly accurate tips for running one's own business. I tell what one can change and how to get to the customer.

8
Do not be afraid to change

Without faith we stumble on a piece of straw.
With faith we move mountains.
Soren Kierkegaard

Every change is a new chance from fate. This is another reason why I am writing this book.

I feel sorry that people cannot use their abilities and do not believe in themselves, they persevere in the belief that the better paid positions are still reserved mainly for the English. The language barrier sometimes seems insurmountable. Why? It turns out that most of girls cleaning and working as a nanny after many years of working in the UK use communicative language, and some of them even advanced English. And this is a promising start.

The same applies to men. It often happens that the boy working as an ordinary worker can communicate better with customers than their Pakistani or Polish manager. What strength traps him in jobs of low wages? Why does he cling to work with the Polish?

I do not know why people are stuck with the same employers, earning minimum wages, even though they know the basics of English? As a contract employee I frequently change jobs, but I use the same network of coffee shops or pubs where I jump out for lunch. Polish people work in every third of them. They communicate quite well in English. I suspect that in addition to doing customer service they are also able to communicate in English with a team of colleagues and a manager.

For the last year I have talked to many Poles and other nationalities, who got stuck in a deadlock, because I wanted to understand the limits of this mechanism. Only a few people have told me that they like what they do, and do not intend or do not want to change jobs. Most of them declare a willingness to change jobs due to earnings, a sense that life is leaking through their fingers, and they still remain in the same place. When asked what prevents them from putting dreams into action, they mention many causes: insufficient knowledge of English, unattractive CV – if they have it at all – and no idea how to look for a new job. One thing is certain: they are not determined people.

And here some readers may be disappointed. There is no easy way to career. Everything depends on ourselves, on our approach, determination and faith – not in miracles, but faith in our own strength! It may be hard to comprehend, but the rush to the front and determination can be earned. Is everyone able to accomplish what they have dreamed of until now? I think so, but they must clearly define the purpose and do not abandon the chosen path. Do not be discouraged by failure.

This is why I decided to share with others my, I hope, valuable experience and tell my story, which for me is very fascinating. Why? Because I have achieved a lot. I have reached for positions that are not dreamed of even by many Englishmen, but I, an average girl from Poland succeeded. On coming to the UK, of course, I had dreams, but I had never thought that I could get this far. Because a human in a foreign country feels uncomfortable. The new environment makes them feel withdrawn, confused, uncertain. The additional ballast is the language barrier!

But I think that my story shows that anything is possible. What I write about, has not only been applied in my life but also in the lives of my friends. The next chapter is dedicated to my daughters, who also – like myself - set the bar high, even though deep down I did not believe that they were able to overcome their weaknesses. Now, I am ashamed that I had doubts. Not only that, I was afraid that by bending them into something that was important to me, and trying to control their lives, I would be responsible for their possible failure. I know it was a huge risk, but it was worth taking it.

9

Children are the wings of man.
My daughters

Children are the wings of man.
Arab proverb

Eldest daughter

I have always told my daughters they have to select a profession where immediately after graduation they can earn good money and never, like me, leave everything to the last minute. I tried to impress upon them that they have great potential and can do in life whatever they want, even to be a doctor. Probably you will think that I am a mother who wants her children to fulfil her own ambitions.

And what if they have other plans?

Oh, I've heard. They would like to have the job, they would like doing, and which would bring them pleasure. Well, everyone would like to do exactly what they like, and still make money on it but it is the dream come true, the privilege of very few people who can make their hobby a profitable business. I believe that if we have a very good job, we can afford to implement our passion. I have taught my daughters that medical school has a huge range of possibilities. Medical graduates will always find a well-paid job after graduation. Private practice allows to set flexible working hours and free time devoted to favourite classes. With financial resources, they will be able to fulfil even the most expensive hobby. That is why I have tried to encourage them to study medicine and dentistry. Our conversations on this topic ended usually with an argument. They do not like biology (especially in English), and they detest chemistry. Not only that, my elder daughter really is afraid of blood.

However, as I mentioned in the previous chapter, to my surprise, both opted for these subjects and physics at their A levels. I was afraid they did so in order to please me, not because of the opportunity to study the medicine. As they said, this profession was reserved for highly talented people – let's call them by name – geeks.

I follow a certain principle – trying to effect. Sometimes you have to find a way to do it. I decided to prove (to myself and my off-spring), that impossible is nothing. I had to act. First, I decided to work on my elder daughter. She did not want to hear about medical profession, regardless of specialty. Tinkering in the human body frightened her, she was indeed aware of the activities in the dissecting room, which she would not be able to bear. She also thought of dentistry as disgusting. I heard more than once NO SUCH OPTION! "Well, we'll see." I took it as a challenge, perhaps one of the greatest in my life.

Malvina was eager to go to work for a day or two a week to have her own money. Despite my great earnings, and Jacek's pretty good earnings, we did not give the girls large pocket money. Any gadgets and technological innovations they got very late compared to their peers, therefore Malvina needed her own money. She was determined and she wanted to find a job close to home, so as not to waste time commuting. I remembered that Jacek used to install an alarm system and cameras at a nearby dental clinic. Immediately, he went there to ask the owner, a dentist, to see if they needed someone to help. Of course, he highlighted the whole situation. It turned out that the doctor was just looking for a worker, it was true, for someone qualified, but for some time he could use any help.

In the evening, we asked our daughter to talk with us and told her that Jacek had just learned about the work near home, but surely she would not want it. Malvina jumped with joy. She wondered why we thought she would not want the job. And we replied that in the dental office nearby there was a vacant place for some time, but while Jacek was talking with the owner, he showed no interest thinking that Malvina would not want to work there.

My daughter winced, but the desire for earnings won. She said graciously, she could go there to try for one day, but in advance she warned that if she saw the doctor digging around in somebody's mouth, it might upset her stomach, and when she would see blood, of course she would faint. Yes, she could work at the reception desk, but certainly not in the consulting room! We agreed and our daughter began her first day of work on Saturday. I knew that it was 'there and then' if she would decide whether or not she was actually suitable for becoming the doctor and if this profession might interest her.

She returned after seven hours tired, but we did not notice that she was unhappy. She did not say anything. We asked if we could already call the doctor with the information that she would not come to work anymore. Attention, attention! Amazingly, my daughter said she would probably go to the clinic once again next week. Hm, could she swallow the hook? The next week, she also went to work twice.

Not to prolong my story, I would say briefly, she worked there for three years until we moved out of London. The doctor liked her very much, and every six months he gave her a raise. She worked interchangeably with a dental nurse employed on a permanent basis. To this day, Jack has been laughing at this intrigue. Not once did she faint at the sight of blood. Later, she admitted on the first day she had to help the doctor with the patient, and he taught her how to name every tooth and prepare the filling. And it was not a problem. In the summer she worked a few days a week. During the first months of work she said that in the future she would like to become a dental nurse, but as she began to work with tools, sometimes helping the doctor she realised that assisting was not enough for her and probably she would make a good dentist.

She knew, however, that there still was the matter of studying for A Levels. Could she get to Uni and complete it? She had huge doubts. So did I. I have to admit.

Younger daughter

I wondered what stratagem to apply to the younger daughter to direct her onto the right track, too. She was not so much afraid of blood, but since she was little girl she had been pedantic and everything was always in order. She liked the cleanliness, she used antibacterial hand gel all the time, and contact with someone else's saliva disgusted her. It did not matter, she would work in rubber gloves. She watched series CSI passionately, but never showed a desire to become a doctor.

It turned out, however, that Daria probably envied Malwina because she asked my elder daughter's employer about the possibility of holding a free school practice at his clinic. The doctor, of course, agreed. She liked very much working at the doctors, he was also pleased – his surgery gleamed, having been perfectly cleaned, everything was sorted. Even patients' catalogues were arranged in order. Daria went to the clinic to replace Malvina many times.

I was over the moon.

Well? Who was right? We cannot say that we are not good for something, if we did not try to do it, or that we do not like something, but we never really had a chance to find out about it the hard way.

I knew that this was only half the battle. The biggest challenges were still ahead of my daughters: they would have to get accepted to a Uni, and then manage with studying. But they admitted I was right. Had they not attempted, they would never have been convinced that they could do something like that. Nay. This profession genuinely interested them.

And what happened next? You will read about this in the next part of the book.

10
SWOT

Twenty years from now, you will be more disappointed with what you did not do, than with what you did. So, leave the safe haven. Catch the trade winds in your sails.
Travel, dream, discover.
Mark Twain

For a start it is worth realising what limits us. What really makes us stay where we are, and why we do not move forward? Is it just a matter of fluency in English? Were we confident and open to a change in Poland? Is it just a matter of lack of confidence which deprives us of any desire to act? Do we know what we are good at, are we aware of our weaknesses and strengths? Where are we going now, and what do we really want to reach? Is there any one of you with hand on heart who can say they did this analysis of their own life?

Everyone has the list of things to do. I am not talking about the usual mundane matters. I mean issues that we took a back seat to and they were really on the list of things "not to achieve." For various reasons, we did not undertake any action or after a few steps, we gave up.

To be successful, you have to engage yourselves 100% in everything you do, not give up once you've chosen a path. The principle is simple – where there is a will, there is a way. If you think that you can do something by half-measures, you are wrong.

Below I will present SWOT analysis, probably already known for some of you, which applies not only to a business plan but it is also used to study the human personality.

A little theoretical information

A SWOT analysis enables the collection and sorting of data and its clear presentation. It is a strategic tool used to determine the best development directions of the object, for example a company, project, venture or idea – in this case – our personal development.

A SWOT analysis can be carried out in many ways. The simplest and most widely used is to identify factors that may affect the functioning of the object (ourselves) and segregate them into four groups:

Strengths – S (Strengths) – an internal factor (characteristic of the object), or anything that can advantageously contribute to the development of our project and is largely dependent on us. They are our strengths and advantages – and strengths, if used in a proper way will promote our development. They represent an advantage over the competition thanks to our experience, knowledge or skills.

Weaknesses – W (Weaknesses) – an internal factor (characteristic of the object), or what is our weakness or a barrier to development, what limits us. It is also a lack of sufficient qualifications, poor organisation of career paths, lack of motivation, that is, those factors that impede the effective operation and success. If we do not eliminate or if we do not offset the impact of these characteristics, they will impede our development. The more weaknesses we write out, the better chance to succeed we have.

Opportunities – O (Opportunities) – an external factor (characteristic of the environment), which is what gives us the chance for positive change, conditions that, with skilful use, can positively influence the development of our career. The multiplicity of our abilities, which our competition does not possess, the idea of self-promotion during the interview, our further development on the work market, i.e. our ideas and emerging opportunities.

Threats – T (Threats) – an external factor (characteristic of the environment), which is what gives us the danger and adverse effects. Factors which do not paralyse our actions now, but they can be a big threat to our future career, for example, increase of the number of people with similar qualifications, competition on salaries, costs caused by moving out in search of work. All the changes, which are able to negatively affect the implementation of our plans and do not depend on us.

11
Your personal SWOT analysis

*Always work your way to the top. You can achieve
everything you want,
but first you have to figure out who you are, and go to work with
a higher power than you can imagine.*
Ella Wheeler Wilcox

SWOT analysis is a very flexible tool, the effectiveness of which really depends on your imagination and creativity. It is used in discovering your own weaknesses and potential. It often opens your eyes to new opportunities and threats, helps to systematise your knowledge of the subject and sense on some issues.

We have already established that each of us has strengths and weaknesses. Very often, however, we do not think about them. We hide our imperfections and do not use our potential. Becoming aware of your strengths and weaknesses is the first step in your transformation and personal evolution, and thus the beginning of your success in your career. It is important to work on your weaknesses from the beginning, to define them properly and fearlessly take on new challenges. First, you should know yourself, and it is a long process, consisting of gathering information about yourself.

Often to do proper and thorough SWOT analysis we will need wider knowledge. Its source can be:

Internet – (a huge, unappreciated potential), where you can find all the information about the job market, the best-paid jobs, all courses improving your competence, career development, etc. A mine of information will be blogs, career development sites, forums and other sites containing current information on market demand.

Friends – also an underestimated source of information about ourselves. It is worth talking to them about how they perceive us, what they like about us, what we stand out at and what they see as our weaknesses. Let us listen to their advice and thoughts.

Literature – all the books about training and personal development.

How to perform SWOT analysis
To perform the analysis, it will be enough to have a sheet of paper (preferably A3), which is divided into four parts. Below I put examples of questions and issues that can be included in SWOT analysis:

My strengths:

What can I do well?

What are my main assets?

What are the assets that others perceive in me?

How do I use my assets?

Can I develop them?

What can I tell you about myself to my prospective employer about my skills, education, suitability for the position I am applying for?

What makes me different from others? What am I better at than others?

How does my environment perceive me?

What are my personality traits? Am I the type of leader? Can I work in a team?

What are the strengths others perceive in me?

Which professional and private achievements am I most proud of?

If I start something, how big is my passion?

How can I deal with crisis situations?

Am I motivated?

How focused am I on the target?

What knowledge do I have (acquired not only in schools)?

What are my skills?

What is my experience?

My weaknesses:

What am I most afraid of?

Which of my qualities bothers me at work?

How do I deal with the worst?

What am I weak at?

How do other people perceive my weaknesses?

How do I fight my weaknesses?

What are the tasks /activities that I would rather avoid, because I am not sure if I would be able to do them well?

What do my friends consider my greatest weakness?

Are my education and skills appropriate to perform the work which I am applying for?

My flaws. Am I punctual? Do I know how to work under time pressure?

Are there in my surroundings people who have better abilities to be successful?

Which of my weaknesses limit the most my desire to succeed?

Do I lack enthusiasm?

Did I miss resistance for problems?

Do I lack motivation?

Do I lack knowledge?

Do I lack the skills and experience?

My chances:

What new opportunities do I have that are opening up for me?

What changes appeared around me?

What occasions that I missed but can I still benefit from?

What trends can become an opportunity for me?

What local events can help me in the development?

Do I rub shoulders with people who have the experience and skills that I am missing?

What the market trends do I observe in my region? Are new companies set up, or shops with the industry, I am familiar with? Are companies increasing employment currently?

Are there in my business market niches that no one fills in? How can I develop what I have done up till now (cleaning, construction industry)?

What are my ideas? Can I make my service unique.

How can I compete with the competition? Have I examined the environment? What services and products are missing around me?

Do I have a chance to cooperate with others?

Can I win investors?

How well did I estimate the initial situation?

My threats:

What obstacles can stand in my way?

Are demands on the employees changing in my current job?

Do technology changes threaten my position?

Do I have financial problems which I have to resolve quickly?

Can any of my weaknesses be a real threat to achieve the goal?

What obstacles do I encounter in my current job or in looking for a job?

Is the demand for employees with my education changing?

Is the number of people with similar skills threatening my career?

Do I not duplicate the errors or other people's ideas?

Do I recognise the competition well?

Does anyone not offer similar products or services in the area?

Can I see the prospects of cooperation with others?

Did I recognise the initial situation well?

Analysis of the above four groups of factors has to build a strategy and – if necessary – the introduction of radical changes needed to strengthen your position in the labour market. A detailed analysis of your capabilities and capacities will be used to determine your own potency to succeed. Especially, being aware of your strengths and weaknesses is crucial in shaping the appropriate strategy, which you are going to apply in the short or long term. It is no secret that the person who has more powerful features than the weak ones has a lot more possibilities – compared to their competitors – to use the opportunities created by the environment and strengthen the position on the work market.

After completing the analysis you will know your strengths and weaknesses. Remember that it depends on you, if you remain forever with your weaknesses, or if you work on yourself and effectively take a chance, you will eliminate the threats.

It is important that you have made the first step towards the change. The effect will depend only on you. It is you who must decide if you will make use of the conclusions of the analysis in order to improve your own personality and succeed. Everything must be done systematically and always lead to personal growth. It will also be easy for you to be able to actually determine in which areas you can achieve success, and in which you will fail. You will be able to determine what features and capabilities you will need to develop in order to succeed and in which direction any changes should be made.

So, shall we do the analysis?
I am aware that this is a very difficult ability to honestly and objectively evaluate your own strengths. But before you start looking for a particular job and prepare your resume, you need to know specifically what you have to offer your potential employer, and whether you are on the right track for a planned career. You need to objectively examine your competence in many areas, such as language fluency, knowledge, skills, creativity, motivation. On the basis of the results it will be much easier for you to narrow down your job search, and determine which job is most appropriate for you, taking into account your skills and personality. Getting to know yourself will make you aware of what you really want to do. If you do not have any particular profession, it will help you choose such one that you

want to learn and train in the desired direction. The analysis of the experience and achievements from the period of work in Poland and then in England, at the professional and personal level, I am sure, will be helpful. As I mentioned earlier, it is worth asking friends, relatives and co-workers about your strengths and weaknesses. Their objectivity and constructive criticism will be very helpful for you.

The first step, therefore, is a precise demarcation of the target for which you will consistently pursue. You need to know what you are really looking for and expect, because otherwise it will be hard for you to define the desired profession and see if it corresponds with your competence, your strengths and personality. Among people prevails the conviction that in today's UK labour market there is a huge competition, therefore they have to accept any job offer, even if it does not correspond to their expectations and is not compatible with their skills. We know perfectly well that most of you work below your qualifications, usually due to poor fluency in the English language.

Therefore, taking the first steps on a career path, take your time and pay attention necessary for such actions as:
- the analysis of strengths and weaknesses,
- the determining of the field in which you want to work and where you have the greatest chance of finding a dream job,
- the determining of the target and the persistent pursuit of its accomplishment,
- undertaking personal development, working on your strengths and competencies,
- developing and acquiring new skills, if the lack of practical work experience prevents you from starting a new career path.

Note – let us be frank and honest
Analysis of your own personality is not easy, especially confrontation of your own observations and conclusions with

assessments and opinions of others. People often underestimate the opinion of themselves, not realising that they can achieve much more. On the other hand, it happens that we overestimate our own ability. Very high self-esteem can lead to disappointment in the future. Fooling ourselves, ignorance of our weaknesses can distort the image of the analysis and will not allow to draw the desired conclusions, which leads to the creation of false picture of the current state of affairs. You cannot overestimate or assign a potential that you are not fully capable of. A bit of self-criticism would be in this case indicated. But this does not mean that you will never enter into possession of the desired characteristics. Everything can be earned.

That is why it is so important to engage yourself 100% in everything that you do. While performing SWOT analysis, it is very easy to make a mistake in your assumptions, and their interpretation. Most often it happens to people preparing SWOT for the newly formed company. Being full of optimism, people overestimate their ability and what they remain with, choking on the vision of the company's success in the market. Therefore, it is important to have an objective approach, commitment and rationalism, as well as cool and thorough verification of your ideas and way of development, identification of deficiencies and greatest strengths. As a result, your plans will be better judged, and you will easily find the best solution and course of action leading to the goal by minimising the risk, limiting the weaknesses, taking opportunities and utilising your strengths.

You need to clearly define what distinguishes you from the competition, so as not to duplicate the same stereotypes. There are a lot of people who say there are no jobs in the UK. I disagree with this opinion as work is available, regardless of the crisis. You just need to try more and act outside the box, avoiding disappointment and discouragement. You have to keep your eyes and ears wide open and clearly define any further step, but also the target group of people who will give you the job (agencies and employers), because your success depends on your contact with them.

12

Your GREAT PLAN for the next five years

To be successful, you have to work smart, never give up, but above all you should cherish your magnificent obsession.
Walt Disney

I suggest to allocate for this purpose a not-too-thick notebook (unless someone is fulfilled by writing a diary). You will sketch out your plan in it, say, for the next five years. This is a very long time, so you do not have to stress out that you will not manage to do something in time. Of course, you will be pleasantly surprised if you fulfil the plan in a shorter period of time. While writing it out, take into consideration your goals and aspirations, and already carried out SWOT analysis. Your plan is a long-term project where the goal may be the job position or working in a particular company or achieving certain earnings – or all together. It is important to outline a clear path step by step. Do not leave out any of the smallest stages. The plan must be very detailed, so that you can enjoy even small achievements. This will give you new heart.

Here is a diagram of a very simple plan, which I used to a certain stage:

MY GREAT PLAN

That's what I achieved so far:

Poland:
Education:
Courses:
Odd jobs:
Full-time work:
Gained experience:
Achievements:
UK:
Education:
Courses:
Odd jobs:
Full-time work:
Gained experience:
Achievements:

What do I plan to achieve within the next five years?:

1. Start learning English:
   – how and where?

2. What are the courses I want to do?
   – supplementary ones
   – professional ones
   – higher education
   – and obtain grants

3. Strengthen your resume:
   – volunteering
   – working in local companies

4. Looking for work professionally:
   - to prepare for an interview
   - registration and meeting in job agencies
   - reading guidebooks
   - find the first serious work

5. Analyse your GREAT PLAN at some stage:
   - a possible change of the industry
   - new necessary trainings

6. Find employment in a thriving company:
   - private pension
   - private medical insurance
   - the possibility of free training

7. Change the company for a better one

8. Open your own business

After five years:
I am no longer threatened by unemployment because with acquired skills I can easily find work in the position of xxx with earnings from xxx to xxx.

13

Education is the passport to a career

Those who win – never ease off.
Those who ease off – never win.
Vince Lombardi

Trainings and education undoubtedly facilitate career development. However, I know people who have gone very far without investing in education. There is one issue – for some people, even education is not a sufficient incentive to ensure moving up the ladder with determination. I know people who, despite their qualifications got stuck or pursue their goals with very small steps, for fear of failure.

You have probably already guessed that I am going to give you some examples.

When I was still a freshman, neither I nor the other students looked for a job. We had a lot of studying, and the beginning of study was very hard. But already in the second year we started looking for some occupations. I did not understand why the majority of my mates found employment in restaurants, bars, pubs. When friends asked me where I offered my CV, I said that I was looking for office work, and of course they tried to convince me that I had no chance of getting such job and would be bitterly disappointed. Before graduation, I could look for work in a shop only. Of course, I was of a different opinion and, as you know, I finally got my first dream job in the Attractions.

For my friends it was unthinkable. They really could not believe that everything happened the way I wanted. They were full of admiration that I dared to register with employment agencies and I immediately ran for ambitious jobs corresponding to the faculty I studied in. In turn, I was surprised that they valued themselves so low and did not see even a hint of a chance of finding another job apart from in a restaurant. Young talented people of different nationalities, with British citizenship. Why did they not want to reach out for more? After all, they were studying such a great faculty as Accounting. This is the reason to be proud of. Where is the belief in self-confidence? In the end, it was me who was the foreigner without UK citizenship. At least they could give it a try.

When I worked in the Attractions, I met with another example that people felt the blockade from taking courageous steps. They kept telling themselves, that their career should start from the lowest of positions in the hierarchy and laboriously climb up the career ladder.

It does not have to be like that.

Every morning, I commuted to Attractions by bus. The bus stop was some three hundred metres away from my company office, therefore, at nine o'clock each morning everyone usually walked to work in groups. Many people worked in various positions in the office building which housed the headquarters of Attractions. Usually, I was accompanied by a boy a lot younger than me, who graduated less than a year earlier. He liked to talk to me. One day he told me his story, and I liked that I did not fail to give him a reprimand and a lot of tips for his career. Well, James was a very talented young man who graduated in biochemistry from the best possible result, at that time he used to work as a telephone ticket salesman for London Attractions. He asked me how many years it took me to find such a good job that I was doing then. Well! I was so satisfied! I explained him using my imperfect English, I was in the second year of study, but never in my life would it come to mind to look for work not related to the field that I studied. I asked James what recruiters told him in agencies when he was looking for employment in laboratories and clinics. Of course, it turned out that he did not even ask for such work. Why? He began to explain that one had to start somewhere, somehow to fill in CV. I understood he had to make a living, but I think there is nothing to prevent that CV to be submitted to the agency and lay in a drawer of a recruiter with the appropriate note on biochemistry!? With such good results of studies James could apply for a trainee position or apply for voluntary work in the laboratory once or twice a week, or to apply for the opportunity to undergo trainings in both private companies and the state ones.

My daughter has not yet completed even a college, and has already received calls from employment agencies and offers of work in the lab, which constantly needed replacement for different employees. Of course, it is not research, but helping in the preparation of the test tubes, but this is a good start of a professional career. My daughter admittedly has not ever used of these proposals, but it confirms my theory that such positions are available, and he who seeks shall find.

Another example, already known to you. After graduating from university I had – and still it happens – a lot of phone calls from students conducting a survey. I am still asked about my career and about how I found my first job. Very often, they did not want to accept that one can start looking for their dream job right away. I told them also that they had to look for it properly. First, start looking, secondly, keep going and do not give up.

I will quote now another story, very close to me because it confirms the theory that the lack of education is not any barrier, and that even from the failure one can rise in style.

On the first organisational day of studies, I met a Polish girl named Iza. It was a nice, fairly secretive girl, she did not like to fraternise with others. I was able to make her talk more openly with me. I learned she had enrolled economics because she did not know what to choose. I managed to convince her to decide to switch to my field of study Accounting & Finance. She was very happy, because she had considered the possibility of working in the financial industry or accounting. In Poland, she started to study economics, but it did not work out for her. She was glad that by studying at our faculty, she could get nine exemptions to the ACCA. Previously, she had no idea about it. You could say that I and Iza became friends, even though she was eight years younger than me. She came from a dysfunctional family, and nothing in life came for her easily. In the UK she had already been for quite a long time, she worked as a babysitter and cleaned up houses.

I noticed that she attached great importance to money. Moreover, she had already set aside a pretty good amount, I am sure it would have sufficed for a deposit on a house. She worked from dusk till down. I was full of admiration for her hard work. It reminded me more of the work period in Poland: three jobs and children on my head. She still had no children.

I have already mentioned to you that the first year at the university was very difficult and it was necessary to devote time to study intensively. Iza did not always appear on the seminars, because she did not want to lose clients and money of course. The effects did not have to be waited for long. From the first session she had two exams to retake, from the second one the next ones. The next year she began with a backlog. Constantly, I was repeating to her that she could use the money which she had set aside to be able to focus on learning. She took a student loan. It seemed to her, she would manage, she would be able to finish her studies, work and simultaneously put money aside. My explanation, that the funds invested in the study would quickly pay off after graduation, were good for nothing. She had to repeat the whole second year, to no avail. She never stopped working.

Nevertheless, after unsuccessful studies she decided to seek her good fortune in the employment agencies and work in her dream profession. Thanks to a few passed exams she gained three credits covered by the ACCA certification.

Agencies began to send her to interviews. Sometimes, we prepared for them together. Iza had usually been employed as a Purchase Ledger Clerk or Account Assistant. After some time, she was trying to find a job in the bank. And, surprisingly, she did not even have to emigrate outside London, as I did. She received employment in an investment bank. Her contracts were not long indeed, from one to three months, but considering the failure in Uni (though understandable), she was doing quite well. Sometimes, she only mentioned that she wished she had longer contracts, and the best full-time work in the bank.

I can tell you that now she works in Dubai. She started from the job in a commercial company, where, unfortunately, she went through a small hell, because her colleagues were not too kind to her. After a year, she started working at the bank, and now she works in a large oil company and is in the seventh heaven, given that her bank account is bursting at the seams (earnings excluding tax). It seems to me, she does not think about continuing her studies at all. But I am not surprised, she finally achieved what she wanted, and all that without university degree.

Another of my friends I met in London also tied her career to accounting. She had not studied accounting earlier and had not completed any directional courses. Poor English skills made her looking for a job in the Polish-speaking companies. She walked from one Polish accounting firm to another one – and in London they are plentiful – until she found work, at first half-time and then full-time. Alongside, in the evenings she attended college classes in English. After two years of work and study she moved to the English company. She currently runs her own business and is doing ACCA certificate and her customers are both Polish and English. She is doing great.

But there are those who, despite tangible evidence that it is worthwhile to seek ambitious work, they doubt success.

When I graduated, my old classmate Renata contacted me through the Polish social network OUR CLASS. She was not one of my friends, because she always behaved as if she had all the answers. But so many years had passed that I did not even remember that. We arranged to meet at my apartment. At the beginning, she did not say about herself anything, and I did not ask. But after the second glass of wine, people are getting more forthcoming. It turned out that she had come to the UK a few years earlier than I did, after a stormy breakup with her boyfriend, and that she cleaned up houses for very wealthy clients. I reciprocated her with the story about myself. I had just finished University and started my career, so I did not really have anything to boast about. But she went speechless, especially when she found out what I had studied. She stammered that the Poles were never paid as much as the British after such studies and it did not make any sense to spend so much time learning, because we would always be underpaid. Oh my, where could she have read that? Why such nonsense? I admitted to her that my earnings so far had not been impressive, but I was happy. She tormented me so long that I told her what incomes I really achieved. During this period, I earned about £22,000 per annum. She went speechless the second time. She said I was paid like an English person! And then she confessed she studied AAT once, but after a year and a half, left school because she could not see the point. She said, in such a situation she was immediately going to come back on her course to finish it.

It was all ridiculous for me. If she had completed the AAT then, she would be far ahead from me now, with richer professional experience and higher wages.

After a few months we met again. At that time, she studied for the next stage of the course, but then did not start the next one. Her enthusiasm was over. But she was with me in constant contact to keep track of my career. When I got another job with a rate of more than £14 per hour, instead of congratulating me, she said the agency probably cheated me and so I would not get such money. I was not going to argue with her. As you know, the agency did not fool me.

You will not believe what happened when I got the job in Jersey for £18 per hour. Again, she started to continue to study

AAT. But when I returned from exile contract, it turned out that once again she left school.

You have to imagine how I motivated her when I started my career at a daily rate in banks and bought my first house. Renata, after thirteen years in England, still cleaned houses and was not able to buy even the smallest property. The problem was not the acquisition of the deposit, but getting a loan. When I bought another property, she returned to the AAT.

At the moment, I have no contact with her and I do not know whether this is because she is so busy with work and study, or simply does not want to admit that once again she gave up the course. She has lost so many years.

There are people who simply cannot be helped, even though they have been shown the right way. Renata herself once chose the right direction, but could not hold on to it. She was not convinced even by my financial achievements, but every time we met up, she made plans to buy her own apartment. Such a shame. I am not going to wait until I am sixty-five years old to retire.

14
Training

*Success seems to be largely a matter of persevering when
others give up.*
W. Feather

The choice of training courses depends on the way of a career
chosen by you. I introduce to you a few options – I guess that I
do not hit all the expectations, but later you will be able to ask
me questions via my website if you express the desire to register
for it. I will keep updating my site with new courses and the
prospects for a career in various fields.

Accounting
Accounting is a sector that gives a lot of chances of financial
success. A lot depends on how much time you can devote to
learning and on your financial resources. The best known are:
AAT, ACCA and CIMA.

I recommend AAT to people who prefer to move forward
with small steps and are aware that they will need more
time to study because they are not especially gifted in the
field of accounting.

This of course does not cancel your chances for the successful
completion of courses, and of finding a job as an accountant.
An additional plus – the English language is from a completely
different field. In contrast, I recommend ACCA and CIMA to
people who feel adventurous and want to bite the bullet.

Option One: Association of Accounting Technicians (AAT)
AAT courses, or AAT Accounting Qualification, are courses in accounting and finance. There are many institutions and colleges which offer this type of trainings. The study is divided into three levels.

- *Introductory – AAT Level 2 Certificate in Accounting* – basic level. After completing this level you can work as: Accounts Administrator, Accounts Assistant, Accounts Payable Clerk, Bookkeeper, Payroll Administrator, Payroll Officer, Purchase / Sales Ledger Clerk, Tax Assistant / Trainee, Accounts Trainee Technician. As for earnings, you can expect from £8,000 to £22,000 per annum.

- *Intermediate – AAT Level 3 Diploma in Accounting* – the level more advanced, after which you can work in the occupations of (Level 2) and additionally as: Expenses Supervisor, Assistant Accountant, Audit Trainee, Corporate Recovery Analyst, Credit Controller, Finance Assistant, Insolvency Executive , Practice Bookkeeper & Payroll, Tax Accountant. Earnings similar from £11,000 to £22,000 per annum.

- *Advanced – AAT Level 4 Diploma in Accounting* – the most advanced level. It opens the door to the following professions: Assistant Financial Accountant, Commercial Analyst, Cost Accountant, Fixed Asset Accountant, Indirect Tax Manager, Payments & Billing Manager, Payroll Manager, Senior Bookkeeper, Senior Finance Officer, Senior Fund Accountant, Senior Insolvency Administrator, Tax Supervisor, Tax Accountant. Earnings from £12,000 to £26,000 per annum.

Of course, it is not true that at the completion of Level 2 you could not find a job as an Assistant Financial Accountant.

Everything depends on how you look for a job. If you know what you care about, and you focus only on that, there is no obstacle when just starting AAT course in finding a job as a trainee. There is a chance that the employer will finance you the whole course of AAT. Therefore, if you are thinking about taking AAT study, I suggest you sign up for a few or several employment agencies and note that you are looking for a job at Entry Level, because you are going to complete the course, and you would need the practice even for a minimum rate (of course, at the beginning).

You can study AAT full-time, part-time and online, in the comfort of your home. Each level takes about a year. But I know people who at one year completed the whole course (fast track). The cost of the first course is £600 to £1,000, plus registration fees to the AAT. It is advisable to choose the school that offers financing studies and helps in getting accepted to a college. Recently I have learned that it is possible to obtain a so-called 24+ Loan. It is open for persons over twenty-four years of age who have been the UK residents for three years. The loan is available for Level 3 and Level 4. Completion of Level 4 is the equivalent of finishing the first year of study. If you compare this qualification to the ACCA qualification, you will find that having completed the AAT, you have gained three passes entitling to acquire certification ACCA F1, F2, F3. Go ahead, you can begin the next phase of training and try to win the next ACCA certificate.

Option Two: The Association of Chartered Certified Accountants (ACCA).

This is an association recognised worldwide, bringing together professional accountants. ACCA courses – as I have already mentioned – are not easy. It is quite a big challenge to prepare for exams, fees for preparatory course and the cost of training materials. Tuition is approximately £1,300 and includes the main course, revision course and preparation for exams course. If after the first course (the cost about £500) you feel energetic enough to take the exam, you do not have to sign up for all three courses. The price of exams is about £70, but if you decide to take the exam at the last minute, it may be even £226.

Examinations are held twice a year in June and December. At one time, you are allowed to sit three exams. ACCA courses are divided into two levels: Fundamentals and Professional. Fundamentals is an introduction to Financial & Management Accounting Techniques and includes mainly technical issues, which all Accountants must master to perfection. Professional level is based on the already well-established knowledge and enriches it with advanced skills and tools.

The **ACCA** course consists of the following stages:

Fundamentals Knowledge
F1 Accountant in Business
F2 Management Accounting
F3 Financial Accounting

Fundamentals Skills
F4 Corporate & Business Law
F5 Performance Management
F6 Taxation
F7 Financial Reporting
F8 Audit & Assurance
F9 Financial Management

Professional Essentials
P1 Governance, Risk & Ethics
P2 Corporate Reporting
P3 Business Analysis

Professional Options (two to be completed)
P4 Advanced Financial Management
P5 Advanced Performance Management
P6 Advanced Taxation
P7 Advanced Audit & Assurance

To become a full member of ACCA (fully qualified), you need to complete the first nine levels, F1 to F9, and complete an online module Ethics, then gain three years of professional experience, and fill in an online list of thirteen of the twenty Performance Objectives and of course also pass two more tests, Professional Options. In total, you should complete fourteen exams.

I think if someone does not have time to waste and is very determined, they should immediately opt for ACCA, because with each exam their earnings will grow, provided that they do not get stuck in place.

Surely some of you at this moment doubt the success of such a long-term project. Do not be discouraged by this, no one is perfect. I passed only nine exams necessary for ACCA certification and, as you can see, I am doing great. Of course, I plan to complete further exams, because recruiters of employment agencies from time to time ask me if within the ACCA courses there has been any progress in my education. Meanwhile, I am included as part qualified or qualified by experience. ACCA does not accept this term because both the one who passed only three exams, and one who scored nine exams can say about themselves they are part qualified, but the difference is fundamental. But it is incumbent on the agency to promote us well, regardless of the level of qualifications of a candidate.

The good news is that if you have not studied yet and you do not have higher education or bachelor's degree, by passing ACCA exams you can get a bachelor's degree and higher education. ACCA acts in partnership with Oxford Brookes University. This means that you can get the BSc (Hons) Degree in Applied Accounting while studying which offers exams under ACCA Qualification.

While studying ACCA or after you can count on finding employment at many desirable positions. Their list is very long: Auditing, Tax Consulting, Financial Control, Management Accountancy, Treasury Consultancy, Business Analysis and Entrepreneurship in each sector and in various companies.

Option Three: The CIMA Chartered Institute of Management Accounts.

CIMA similarly to ACCA includes a professional Accounting Program, as well as globally recognised Accounting Qualifications, which require students to gain practical work experience in the field before they are certified.

CIMA is more focused on areas such as Management Reporting (Strategic Planning, Forecasting etc.) and ACCA focuses on competence in the field of Auditing & Tax (Accounting Rules & Regulations). Of course, the two qualifications are highly desirable by employers around the world and allow you to find employment in exactly the same professions. If you want to get a high competence and you are looking for work in the company dealing with accounting or specialising in the type of jobs like tax and audit, then ACCA certification will be more useful. If you dream of working in companies from such areas as Strategic Work (Management Consultancy), CIMA certification will be more relevant. In fact, there is no rule for this. I am the perfect example. I decided to work in banks and companies in the area of Financial Services, and not typical accounting offices, because I do not like bookkeeping, and I have yet the eligibility of ACCA.

Option Four: University – for the most daring ones, but in the end also for all people.

A variant for determined individuals, but also for those having some financial facilities. Of course, you can apply for funding of studies and a student loan, you must pay it off in accordance to your income (if your income exceeds £21,000, the instalments amount to 9% of your salary). With a Student Loan (Tuition Fee Loan), you can receive up to the amount which equals the total fees for college, or up to £9,000, and for the part-time over £6,000. Applications are to be submitted to the Student Services Finance European Team. Grants and maintenance loans to cover the cost of living during studies are unfortunately mainly available for the British, however, I found indication that students from the EU can apply for extra help, provided they have lived in the UK at least for three years, and also for other causes than just studies and if the course qualifies itself for funding: it must have the status of higher education. It is worth verifying the information concerning the offer by individual universities, it happens that they offer additional help. For example, The London School of Economics & Political Science subsidises tuition from £500 (with an income from £40,000 to £42,000 per annum) to £3,500 (income of £18,000 per annum). And most importantly, this aid does not have to be returned.

If you're going to study Accounting & Finance, it is good to choose a university which accredits ACCA or CIMA. Examinations in the individual subjects are automatically recognised by ACCA and you do not have to sit them again to get a certificate, provided that you will gain the appropriate number of points on the exams. The time I went to university I remember as a very difficult one in my life. After all I had a family and children. Until I finished my studies, I felt guilty. I was afraid to look into the eyes of my closest ones, fearing that I was not able to complete the study and that I could let down their trust and faith in me. So if your situation is a little bit better than mine, it is really worth studying. If you are in a worse position, I suggest extramural study to avoid stress and gain more time to learn.

If you plan to invest in education, I recommend lots of different types of study, not only Accounting. There are many interesting faculties that will enable you to fulfil the dream of finding a great job and finally take care of your hobby. My friend has always dreamed of designing clothes and is just finishing the study associated with the design of clothing. The portfolio, which she presented while applying for this course, was not impressive, because as far as ideas for clothes were great, but her drawing skills not so much. She risked and… will soon reach what she has planned. I keep my fingers crossed for her.

Dental nurse
Many people ask me if it is worth finishing a course for qualification to practice as a dental nurse. The answer is clear:

yes, if you want to choose this type of a career in your life. It is also an option for your child if, of course, they are already teenagers. It is advisable to find out if this is an area in which your daughter or son would feel like a duck in water. It is very hard for young people to decide what they want to do in the future.

The earnings of a dental nurse range from £16,000 to more or less £28,000 a year. Of course, this is only the average data from the internet. Working in private practice in a good neighbourhood, you can earn more. Obviously, appropriate courses are necessary. With any luck, the employer is able to send you to a training and even pay for it.

The good news is that you do not even have to have any skills to start a job as a trainee dental nurse, and then start studying part-time (or evenings) in order to obtain a diploma. Each course leading to qualification to exercise the profession of a dental nurse must be approved by the General Dental Council (GDC).

Such courses include:
- NVQ Level 3 Diploma in Dental Nursing.
- NEBDN National Diploma in Dental Nursing awarded by the National Examining Board for Dental Nurses,
- VRQ Level 3 in Dental Nursing.
- QCF Level 3 Diploma in Dental Nursing.
- Certificate of Higher Education in Dental Nursing (full-time)
- Foundation Degree in Dental Nursing (full-time).

Courses take place in dental hospitals, colleges and various organisations. Also, some universities offer full-time courses certified by the GDC. In addition, selected NHS Trusts allow you to gain experience in the field of dental nursing during practice (apprenticeship).

I will not dwell on each course. The most famous is NEBDN National Diploma Course, which offers trainings for the profession of dental nurse fully accredited by NEBDN. Trainee dental nurse can through this course become a qualified dental nurse. After gaining additional qualifications she will gain the opportunity to register with the GDC. Of course, in order to get NEBDN National Certificate, each dental nurse who takes the exams, must also complete a two-year internship in a dental surgery.

And here I will tell you a secret. Even better than the profession of dental nurse can be dental hygienist, dental therapist (oral health practitioners) or orthodontic therapist. Earnings are even two times higher, but to be able to work in such positions you need experience as dental nurse.

When my daughter was working in a dental surgery, she mentioned me about a dental hygienist, for whom the dentist made appointments with patients every Thursday. He wanted to have on offer an additional service of dental services so that patients would not look for them elsewhere. It costs a patient £39 per half an hour. Thursdays were often filled with reservations three weeks in advance. I do not know whether the dental hygienist shared the money with the doctor, but no doubt such a system would bring them mutual benefits. She dealt with the thorough cleaning of tartar (ultrasound), which revealed any new defects, which emerged on a teeth under the liquidated efflorescence. After each treatment the dental hygienist included the relevant annotations in the patient chart.

You will think to yourself: why could not she offer her services twice a week? The answer is simple – dental hygienist is not a popular profession, therefore she was sought-after, and every day she worked with another doctor. The surgery was not large, therefore the dentist did not have the possibility to spend another day on treatments performed by a dental hygienist.

Online courses
Another alternative is online courses, which I recommend. A lot of my friends graduated from these fields of study, which allowed them to retrain.

I recommend the site www.alison.com.

Courses are available in various categories:
- Business & Enterprise Skills
- Financial & Economic Literacy
- Health & Safety & Compliance
- Health Literacy
- Personal Development & Soft Skills
- Digital Literacy & IT Skills
- Diploma Courses
- Health & Safety (Irish Legislation Only)
- Languages
- Schools Curriculum (AAT)

You are probably wondering if they are expensive? Well, the majority (600) are free.

On visiting Reed agency, I advise you check what courses it offers. They are really a lot:
- IT
- Accountancy & Finance
- Admin, Secretarial & PA
- Business & Management
- Health & Care
- Teaching
- Media, Creative & Design
- Trades
- Sports & Fitness

So, we have a wide range of possibilities: from courses for electrician or plumber to a web designer or programmer.

Investing in yourself is the best investment we can make. Do not hesitate then. Additional qualifications add confidence and enhance the value of your CV. Do not worry about minor setbacks. It should also be noted that the lack of qualifications does not cancel your chances of finding a dream job. You just need to properly approach it.

15
English without taboos

Standard education will provide you with experience.
Self-study – a fortune.
Jim Rohn

Once again I repeat: you must be determined to change. I do not expect you will assign yourselves the deadline – the very thought of taking to language learning, which you have been putting off for so long, is stressful. As you know, the book is addressed primarily to those who are ready to face the challenge and learn the English language to the extent necessary to find their dream job. Please do not be discouraged. There are many ways to master the language fairly quickly.

Let me tell you how my friends learned English, using the unconventional ways and tricks. I will also tell you many other – more conventional – methods which are used depending on the degree of advancement of fluency in English. I warn you in advance that some of the methods are fairly mundane, but they are proven and effective.

One of my friends I accidentally met in London (in Ealing in front of the Polish church) learned English using small steps. I met her in the first week of her stay in the British capital. She asked me the way to her first client (cleaning houses), because she had not yet mastered the art of using a map. Well, I explained to her how to get to her destination, but I could not imagine how she could communicate with Mrs Woolf (her employer), because she did not speak English. I will not go into details, I will add only that she currently works as a store manager in a large, well-known shopping centre.

To learn English, she asked Mrs Woolf to put down most of the commands on small sheets of paper and then read them aloud. Later, Magda wrote down the pronunciation but the meaning of words she looked up in the dictionary. She collected all these sticky notes. In her room almost every piece of furniture and equipment was pasted with a yellow sticky note with the name of the object and its pronunciation. The entire notebook was filled with sentences spoken by Mrs Woolf. Three times a week she took her notes for correction and the woman, who was delighted with her work, checked all records and added a few new sentences to learn. After some time, Magda mastered basic phrases and names of objects, which she used at work. Soon Mrs Woolf began to ask her about the details of her life, about school, family, etc., and gradually expanding the subject of conversations in the language of Shakespeare. This type of conversation they practiced for almost two years.

You probably acknowledge that this way of learning a language is very simple and practical. How many of you have signed even half a notebook of your own volition? Magda had one goal: she decided to work as a manager in a large, well-known shop and she was ready to attain this. When Mrs Woolf's children went to kindergarten, and she returned to work, Magda no longer had the opportunity to conduct interviews with clients. In this situation, she used the language during moments spent on shopping, conversing both with vendors and other shoppers. Indians are very friendly, they like the Poles, and always try to maintain a conversation with them. Every night while shopping at the local off-license, Magda chatted with shop assistants. She knew that she would learn to speak English only among the English.

And mainly she would understand what they said to her. Unfortunately, due to financial reasons (commitments in Poland) she could not afford to pay any method of learning the language. After some time, however, she invested in the purchase of a cheap language course in audio form, she could listen to it through headphones, cleaning apartments and houses. It also was a hit!

A little later, she decided to overcome her fears and distribute her so far modest CV in local shops. I helped her write a text that she was supposed to say every time she walked into a store in search of work and to leave her CV. It was not too interesting, but I did my best, it was full of the traits that employers seek in job candidates. Of course, Magda realised her earnings would be lower than the remuneration she received for cleaning, but the benefit resulting from a change in the work was to be invaluable – Magda gained the opportunity to improve her English.

In the end, she managed to get a job in a small boutique with clothes, where at the beginning she unpacked goods, labelled them and hung on hangers. She also managed to create an attractive shop window, which her manager liked very much. The shop girls gossiped a lot, which was certainly beneficial to her, especially since she always had a lot of questions concerning the use of the language. Finally, after several months Magda moved from the warehouse to the store. After some time she changed the place of employment, and though her earnings were still less than satisfactory, the profit was twofold – the girl could boast about better and better language skills, and much more attractive CV. She admitted to me that initially, when a client entered the shop, she prayed that they did not ask her about anything. She still had jitters for a long time. After some time, I lost contact with her, but then I learned from our mutual friends that she worked in a huge shopping center, in a well-known chain stores and she was the head of one of its branches. She was in charge of all orders, preparation of financial statements for the head office and management employees. I am proud of her. Everything she did was subordinated to a specific purpose. She wanted to be successful and get her dream job. I think she would probably stop there. But what do you think: is if she wanted to go further, would she handle that? I know she would.

The most common mistake made by the Poles and other immigrants coming to the UK who are poor English speakers is stereotypical thinking. For this reason, most of them presupposes that the best they could do is to work for a Pole. People are afraid of change, they do not believe that they can get a better position, and that they are able to keep it. But the most important thing is to believe in yourself and find the purpose which then you will consistently pursue. First of all, you need to start to learn the language as soon as you can. It is obvious that not everyone at the beginning can afford to pay for a language course, especially since they just arrived in a foreign country and they are fighting for survival. But the first step after adapting to the new conditions is searching a job in the English environment.

A good example is construction workers employed in Polish companies. It is understood that in a foreign country a Polish colleague generally takes care of a colleague working in the Polish company. However, you have to believe in your strength. If someone performs their duties well and faithfully, each English-speaking employer will accept such a helper or a professional, even if they speak poor English. The possibility of staying in the environment of the living language and using this opportunity to improve it, is the beginning of success. And it only depends on you, what work you will perform in a new country. It is worth considering whether you want to develop in the construction industry, because it is something that you did well in Poland, or rather treat it as a temporary job and try to change the profession. If so, there is no point in wasting time working among your countrymen.

I know this situation from the analysis. I can tell you what Jacek my partner did – a professional computer scientist. He started with the construction industry, but he did not have the thought to seek work with the Poles, though he had some connections. He kept them in reserve, and began submitting applications to English employers. He spoke English on communicative level, like myself, but a collision with the living language is not an easy experience. It makes us realise how little we know this language, how badly we were taught it in Poland and how limited our vocabulary is. By the way: his colleagues knocked their heads, about why he immediately after arrival started seeking employment with British employers. I always kept telling him that he had to stay clear of Polish companies. Not because something was missing, I just knew that the Poles would not teach him English. While working for British companies, Jacek could hone his language. He moved from company to company, until in one of them he started to learn installing alarms and CCTV. He currently owns two businesses: he deals with the programming and installation of home automation. But this is another story. He still has problems with spelling, but he never particularly cared about it. In the end, I am always at hand.

In general, the simplest forms of learning turn out to be the most effective, because they are not so stressful for a foreigner. After a while, you can deliver yourself a higher dose of adrenaline, making several calls a day with the English-speaking callers, for example phone numbers found in the adverts or the Yellow Pages. Sounds weird? I was also full of admiration hearing about the creativity of my friend Sylvia. She worked in a store, and she wanted to get a job in an office. She knew English on communicative level, but realised that even if she would get her dream job, sooner or later a phone on her desk would ring… and she would be the last person who would like to pick it up. She constantly called under different telephone numbers about different weird things to get used to the English language in the realities of a phone call. She called the power company asking if she was not in arrears with payments; to TFL to obtain information on access to the platform for a particular underground station, she called Tesco Clubcard, to be sure how many points she had managed to amass, and so on. At the critical moment she could just hang up. Besides, she had nothing to lose. Funny? I think it is brilliant. To this day, I remember, how difficult it was for me to answer the phone in the dental surgery because of jitters.

But constructive examples do not end up on people with limited knowledge of English, who nevertheless reached their goal and are fulfilled professionally. For ten years I have met a lot of people and heard a lot of supportive stories.

I have already mentioned, this will not be an ordinary book containing the list of theories. I reveal to you the experiences of real people who have passed through my life. I helped some of them, but actually I showed them the way only, and they just believed that if I did it, then they would have to as well! Therefore, I believe that the examples drawn from life can mobilise others to action. Hence the idea for this book. In the UK, there is enough room for everyone. I am not afraid of competition.

Here is the next story which motivated me immensely to write this book. I hope it will mobilise also all those who, regardless of the degree of fluency in English could give the correct course of their life. This story makes us realise how wrong are those who are in their infancy in learning the language and think that people who have excellent English skills have an advantage over them.

At the time when I just started my career, every weekend I visited local shops for clothes. In one of them a young saleswoman asked me: "Can I help you?" Her accent aroused my curiosity. I answered: "I'm fine, thank you." Then she asked directly whether I was Polish (probably my accent was not the best). And so we met.

We went together for coffee and gradually bartered information about each other. Agata had worked in a shop for two years, and it was part-time. For two years she slogged for £6.50 per hour! What's so strange? The fact that the store was lowly, and she had graduated from a three-year college of English in Poland and, as I had seen, spoke good English. I mentioned that I liked to pry into the lives of others, when I saw they did not see any potential in themselves. I immediately slung her with questions what she was doing in that shop, why she did not use the asset of speaking good English, and in addition worked part-time. Her answers were predictable: she did not even look for another job than in a store. They needed someone part-time, and she thought that finding full-time work by a Polish woman was impossible. I was about to finish university then (2008) and I tried to convince her that she had a better chance than I to complete it. It was not clear for her that I was studying in London.

The continuation of the story is as follows – Agata decided to work full-time and after some time she became a store manager. But that is not everything. As I said, everyone can stop at some stage or just go on. Our relationship lasted. Agata was fascinated by the fact that by working in a bank, I gained such great income. As she was not attracted to working in finance, she decided to find a job in a bank in customer service. She served banking customers, who appear in great numbers daily in the bank, to settle various formalities. She got the job after half a year of trying. Working on the front line was not, however, the peak of her dreams. Agata started to apply for jobs in the Head Office of the Bank. In her mind's eye she saw herself at Canary Wharf, working on the contract.

It is good I stood in her way. But for meeting me, Agata probably would not have left her stagnant place quickly. I decided to tell her stories of people I knew which would make her aware of the fact that many people who came to the UK without good English skills had already got ahead her on the way to success long ago, while she with her great English probably would have stayed in a small lowly shop forever.

Currently, Agata works where she wanted to, as an Analyst KYC (Know Your Client Analyst), where she can demonstrate brilliant English in preparation of documents, analysis related to anti-money laundering and risk analysis. The rate is £22 per hour.

As shown by all these stories, contact with the living language is invaluable if you plan to make any career. My example and the experience of my friends illustrates that you can stop at various stages on the way to your destination: the seller in a small shop, or help the dental specialist employed on a contract in the bank at a lower or higher position. The career progression is determined primarily by: determination, self-confidence and persistence, but sometimes success also depends on the extent to which we master the English language.

16
English – courses and training

Without knowledge of foreign languages a person feels worse than without a passport.
Anton Chekhov

Unfortunately, for what you are intending to do, you cannot not miss it. You need to learn English if you are going to succeed. The good news is that you do not need to graduate from English Studies immediately if you want to change your job (unless you plan to be a sworn translator). You should realise the extent to which you must master the English language to be able to work in your chosen profession. One thing is certain: an improvement in language skills is inevitable! You decide if you want to learn English!

I am not going to dwell on conventional methods of learning English because – in theory – we all know them. But do we use them?

Online courses
My friends used online courses and have still benefited from them. I will immediately answer your question: "Where do I get the money from?" Well, a lot of online courses are free. They are addressed to people with varying degrees of sophistication in language skills. I suggest to complete all of them. Of course, to fully use them, you must pass all the stages of the course, from beginner to advanced levels. Do not be disappointed, if you have to go through a stage two or three times. Do not forget to take notes.

The most interesting sites offering online language courses include:
www.alison.com,
www.busuu.com,
www.britishcouncil.org/learn-english.

Of course there are also plenty of websites with payable courses, such as:
www.e-institutelondon.com,
www.eskk.pl.

If you have already taken free courses, it is well worth seeking promotion for paid training. Just register your email address on websites offering language courses, you can be sure that your mailbox will receive information on promotions.

iPod

You could also invest in an English course that you can download on your phone or iPod. Take into account the number of hours spent each day, for example, on cleaning, and you will find that you have at your disposal plenty of time to listen to the course. I know, I know, this is not easy, because cleaning is tedious work and begs for inclusion of rhythmic music and the latest hits. But you can make a deal with yourself: half the time spent on cleaning I will listen to English, and the prize for the second half of listening to music. I realise that it is most difficult to motivate no one but yourself.

College

Another alternative is college. Just type in a search engine, for example: "Learn English in Ealing Broadway" and you will get a full picture of schools available in your area.
www.ealingschooloflanguages.com/
www.a1schoolofenglish.com/
www.ltc-english.com/

You should also go to your local Job Centre to inquire if they offer subsidies or free English courses. Several of my friends took advantage of such an opportunity.

Newspapers

I also recommend reading newspapers. For example, the newspaper *Metro* is publicly available, free of charge and contains articles written in very accessible language. Every day, you should choose a single article and write down from it at least five new words, five times a week. Per year it will be more than thirteen hundred new words !!!

Books

Reading books is priceless. They can be purchased at a very attractive price in charity shops. They do not have to be books for learning English. I learned the language on the detective stories by Agatha Christie. The easiest will be reading children's books. It might be worthwhile to read them aloud to kids? Remember – note down new words!

University

The last option, which I will not describe, of course, is university. To sum up, in order to master the English language, use the following guidelines:
- have permanent contact with English at work,
- do not avoid confrontation with shop assistants in stores,
- perform as many phone calls about variety of simple things as possible,
- have as many English-speaking friends as possible,
- watch English movies without dubbing, only with subtitles,
- listen to your iPod with English-speaking courses,
- read English books (even for kids) and newspapers,
- write out new vocabulary which you encounter daily ,
- use free language courses.

17
First job

Willpower is one of the assets really important in life.
A determined man can get almost everything.
Henry Ford

For some, getting the first job is easy. Many people come to England to visit friends who have already organised them some work. As it is the first work abroad, often not requiring good knowledge of the language, do not be picky and take what fate gives you. There is nothing surprising in this. Stress is huge. I still remember my first call regarding the job in the store advertised in the newspaper and that interview. And London is the place where there is really a lot of work, especially for the unskilled ones and temporary work in very different fields.

I agree with the saying that here the first money is lying on the street (the fact, on the third day after arrival I found £130), you only have to bend down to pick it up. And literally speaking, on every street the first job awaits those who are looking for earnings. In any large and medium or small district there are plenty of coffee shops, shops, restaurants, bars, fast food outlets, takeaways. You say, so what? Maybe two of them have a card in the window that the owner needs someone to work. Well, you are wrong. Especially since I know many owners of such small businesses, and I know that recruitment is always done.

Let me tell you about my friends who came to my place from Poland, in the hope of finding a job. I would add they used the communicative English and intended to find work similar to the one they performed in Poland – of course, to start with a small businesses and lower positions, not just to sit on my hands. I asked how I could help them, but they said that they were prepared for the job search, and by providing hospitality for them I already helped them enough. For two weeks they surfed the internet and sent their CV to potential employers. I was very intrigued, because I could not imagine what their applications looked like. He was a computer scientist, and she was a secretary. I did not want to interfere, it seemed to me, however, that fate was after all impartial and in most cases, we all had to start almost from scratch, regardless of how well we knew the language. I was not surprised that after two weeks my friends began to mutter that a friend of theirs, who had just recently arrived in London, worked in a restaurant, and that no work dishonours. Unfortunately, they had no responses to their CVs.

On the basis of a ten-year observation I know that often those who speak poor English, reach the summit. Those Poles, in turn, who speak English well, often fail to live up to this. I believe that the degree of fluency in the language is irrelevant. What is important is how much you are determined to learn it, and how you want to climb the career ladder, striving to achieve your aims.

My friends tried to skip the first stage, which of course it is understandable – each of us tried. However, the CV of my friends advertised only the position in which they worked in Poland, which probably did not induce confidence in British employment agencies and employers. They expect a CV including an employment history in England. And never mind that you can be proud of such jobs like a builder or help in cleaning. What recruiters are looking for in your CV is confirmation that some British employers have already trusted you, in order to deserve to work in their companies or their homes. It is also important that the prospective employer or recruiter from employment agencies can call for references. It certainly is important, even if the last job you have done was not ambitious. At least it was a job in England.

Finally, my friends decided to look for a simple job, they even realised that they needed to do this out of the house. They decided to look for work in shops and coffee shops. I breathed with relief, finally, there was some progress. Listening to my advice they completely changed their CV. They mentioned in it odd-jobs in Poland (perhaps even from their student days), emphasising what job they were looking for. Having printed twenty copies of their CV (only !!!) they went out to Ealing. They returned in the late afternoon, after they had handed out eight CVs. I almost fainted... The whole of Ealing, only eight CVs???!!! The explanation was simple: in shop windows and the windows of properties they were passing there were not job advertisements. They approached only people who officially were looking for employees.

The mechanism of advertising in street shops or restaurants is very simple. In fact, most do not announce vacancies in the window. You have to enter each company, ask politely to speak to the manager and inquire if you could leave your CV. If he or she is out, just leave your application to an employee of the store. Of course, you should practice at home what you want to say. They are two, three sentences, so even if you know little English, you are able to stammer them. Consistently leaving a CV with potential employers means that most of them do not announce job offers. They have so many applications that they do not have to look for workers. Several times a week someone brings new application. Of course, the pile of CV grows, so every two weeks you should smash them again so that your application is the freshest. In London (and in other cities) every day a lot of people switch from one temporary job to another one.

The next day I went with my friends to Ealing, and together with them distributed their applications. We printed more than a hundred copies of their resumes. I saw how difficult it was for them: to come where into they were not wanted (because of no announcement on the shop window). It is not difficult to guess that many of the CVs landed in the dustbins, but the more applications go to recipients, the greater the chances are of finding the first job. My friends for two more days distributed their CV in other districts.

As I predicted, after some time there was a pretty good response to their applications. He took a job in a coffee shop, and she was for a few days in a restaurant. The fact that hundreds of their CVs were sent to potential employers provided for a much better chance of finding a job. It was not the job of their dreams, but it already gave some financial independence, and thus – the possibility to rent a room.

Sometimes the simplest solutions are the best.

My elder daughter, when she started looking for her first job, even before she started working as a dental nurse, had her own plan of action for me, which was then irrational. One day she told us she had written a CV and was ready to find a job, of course, for a short period of time and part-time. I wanted to help her and insisted that at least I would take a look at her application. It turned out that CV consisted of only half of the page of text, in which she had written her achievements at school and posted a short self-profile. She asked to give her a lift to the local Sports Direct, because there she would like to start her career i.e. work for a few hours a week. I did not want to undercut her wings and explain that this way of job searching might take some time, especially since she had no experience in any industry. I mentioned that she should print at least fifty applications. We nodded our heads doubtfully, but we took her to the store. We waited in the car, discussing how the child was naive. After fifteen minutes she left the store very happy. It turned out she was about to start by the next afternoon.

At the same time, one of my colleagues, a Polish woman, who I met in Uni, sought unsuccessfully part-time work in a shop. She applied for a lot of ads found on the internet. When I told her that my daughter had also began to look for something, full of scepticism, she said that it would be difficult for my daughter to find a job. After all she had sent dozens of resumes and with no effect. And every offer was applied by fifty to a hundred candidates. You should have seen her surprise when, a few days later I boasted that my daughter chose a company located near our home and just immediately got a job.

Thus, my daughter toppled the myth proclaiming that one has to apply online to large chain stores, send cover letters and wait for weeks for a response. The truth is that locally, often even a large network has its own rules and if they need an employee, they will not launch an ad on the internet, as the recruitment process would take centuries, especially as for one ad there are hundreds of applicants. Staff turnover is so high that the cost of ads eventually ceases to pay. And so it is in many industries. Do not fear therefore to provide your CV in person where you just fit and where you want to find a job, regardless of whether they are stores, restaurants or coffee shops. Sometimes the most important thing is to be in the right place at the right time. That friend from Uni took to heart the actions of my daughter – she went to the store with products for animals located near the university and left there her CV. After a week she got a job. She did not waste time on commuting, because after classes she went to work. Well, I can agree with some of you that the two of them were just lucky. But I think we all admit that sometimes luck needs to be helped…

18
Where to find your first job

Empty pockets never held anyone back before taking action.
Empty heads and empty hearts can do this only.
Norman Vincent Peale

Gaining experience, and thus building your CV from scratch, is probably the most difficult process, especially for people who are stuck in one type of work – such as cleaning houses or helping at a construction site – and do not necessarily wish to place this professional experience in their resume. But how to type something more ambitious, if from the beginning of your stay in the UK you have worked only in these occupations? I think there is a solution. Of course, it is worth thinking deeply (I recommend SWOT analysis) about what you want to do and when you intend to achieve your goals. You should also take to learning English immediately in order to be able to freely communicate in the language of your prospective employers and clients.

For a start, turn back in time and recall what profession or what activities you performed in Poland (if you have prepared a plan for the next five years, you have everything exactly as described). If the nature of your work was similar to what you want to do in the UK, you can simply put the employment history of that period in an English CV. If you are looking for an office job and in Poland you did this profession successfully, remember to note down the scope of the duties performed. You want to prove your future boss that you are good for a higher purpose, even though now you are doing something more mundane, like the cleaning or auxiliary work at the site. If you performed a job in the construction industry and you were professional in your field (plumber, electrician), you need to put such references in the application. The same principle also applies to computer science professionals, who are very plentiful in England (including my Jacek). You should also include in your CV the professions done in the home country and include your portfolio in applications. This also applies to many other positions. Your work experience from Poland really counts.

Well, what if during the period that separates the last work done by you in Poland and your current professional status, you only cleaned up houses or worked in the construction sector? Even if by some miracle you will be invited for an interview to employment agencies how you are going to present them this period in your life?

Well, my suggestion is the following: you can put on your resume such episodes as cleaning, dealing with children, ancillary works on the construction site or in a coffee shop, but it is worth noting that this was your first work experience in the UK. I would not advise to elaborate on the details of such mundane duties, you need only to mention them to fill in a short break in your resume forced by emigration.

The first CV should be written in a manner to catch the attention of recruiters from an employment agency or a potential employer with all skills and experience gained by you, and above all it should highlight all the desirable candidate's positive qualities, which you had the opportunity to acquire by working in different occupations and for different employers.

You might ask, what sort of experience one can get by cleaning?

First of all, it is worth noting that the English who employ a Polish cleaning staff bestow great confidence in them, by giving the keys to their homes. A job such as babysitting is one of the most responsible professions, which your employer may offer a stranger. The advantage of such a candidate, therefore, is that it inspires confidence, is honest, diligent and accurate, can work both under supervision, as well as on their own. They can show initiative. They are also patient and communicate on different levels, with children as well as adults (despite poor fluency in English).

If you work on a construction site you should not elaborate all the duties you perform at the behest of superiors, but write about what you are doing on your own initiative. It is important to demonstrate independence, accuracy, ability to communicate with superiors and colleagues, as well as the care and ingenuity.

During a conversation with recruiters from employment agencies or in person with the employer in a very simple way you can highlight the value of this type of mundane work. Even arriving in a foreign country in order to improve skills and language is a bold step on your part, and proves that you are flexible, determined, ready for change and new challenges.

You can point out that after the experience of working in Poland, where you worked in ambitious and widely respected professions, cleaning or working on the construction site turned out to be for you a completely new experience, a challenge and a test for your operability, team skills and adaptability. It is worth noting that the English families who you worked for were very demanding and you gave yourself as accurate and honest employee, since you have been recommended to other employers.

First of all, you need to emphasise, however, that the decision to start working below your qualifications was motivated by poor fluency in English and you needed time to hone the language. You realised that contact with the living language would allow you to master English in communicative level. Hence the idea for cleaning up, dealing with children, working on construction sites, in restaurants and shops. I think nobody will question such a justification. The arguments are strong and often helped my friends to break the barrier among recruiters not wanting to engage in the recruitment process. It is always worth noting that you intend to improve the language on courses or in college. I have used such arguments, looking for a job in the financial industry, when I was in the second year of studies. I included in my CV only the experience, which I could be proud of during the work period in England (working as a dental nurse), and yet I got a job as Assistant to Company Secretary. Recruiters from the agency were amazed that in Poland, I did completely different professions, and here in England, I was a dental nurse without any qualifications and I was good at it. This meant that I will adjust myself to every profession.

The next step is to find another job than cleaning (in case of women) and the construction industry (in case of men). Contrary to appearances, this is very simple. The only argument for to remain in the existing situation is that often the rate for cleaning (£10 per hour) is more attractive than wages in other occupations available for foreigners in a new country (with a rate in the range of £7). This is probably the biggest barrier encoded in the form of a stereotype in our minds. Each of the immigrants usually has the conviction that they came here for a while – a year or two, the top three – to put aside some money and return to their country. Before you know it, five years pass by, and you still are stuck in the same place, happy with the wages and adapted to temporary circumstances. But if at some point you stopped for a moment and took the time to learn the language, self-education or formal education, and then find a more attractive job, your rate after five years would increase to £15 per hour and it is possible that it would gradually be getting higher. You may still consider that you will return to Poland any time. Years go by. Life passes by.

If you do decide to take a lower-paid job – with the idea of it leading to progress in your career – you may find that working all week (excluding weekends) eight hours a day and earning £7 an hour, to reach as much as cleaning up in two places a day, even considering commuting. The first tax threshold is quite high, so full-time work or contracting does not necessarily mean having to pay high tax.

But if indeed someone is able to earn more or a lot more – and I know such people who watch other people's children from morning to evening – there is no way they will want to give up such income in favour of work bringing lower earnings despite it allowing for personal and professional development. I must point out that this book is not addressed to people satisfied with their situation. They will not find neither the motivation nor arguments to abandon their current job.

As for the young Poles working on construction sites, I think the only thing stopping them from pulling out of a small and developing Polish company is the fear of finding a new job and the challenge of communicating in English. I think, however, that they do not have to fear changing their rates for worse. On the contrary – their income may be even greater. English companies appreciate more careful, conscientious and clever employees, moreover, working for an English employer allows for professional and personal development.

The Poles who treat construction industry as a transitional stage, for example, computer scientists, do not have to fear a lower rate as a result of finding a better job, because the function of the helper on the construction site is not well paid. Any change can only turn for good, contributing to the more rapid finding of a job in their profession.

But back to the topic.

You already know how to convincingly demonstrate front of a potential employer the benefits of cleaning the home of the English or granting to the construction site. Now it is time for a change. You may find that you do not have to give up the work entirely.

The best way to change your current state of affairs is to find a local employment agency. I mean even a small branch of Reed, Adecco or any other agency. You can search for them on the internet by typing in a search engine the name of a particular district. These types of agencies often offer temporary work for one day or a few days.

This is how my friend Danusia found a job. For almost three years she had cleaned houses in Ealing. I met her by chance. She replied to my ad on the internet. I had plenty of plush toys and a lot of cool, undamaged clothes after my daughters grew up, and I wanted to get rid of them for free. She called and said she would take everything willingly. It turned out that not for her daughter, who was, as my girls, a teenager. Danusia wanted to send them to the Poland, to her neighbour, who raised five children by herself. And so we met. She told me about her dreams and in a fit of candour she confessed that nothing good would probably await her. She was stuck in London, cleaning here for a couple of years, while in Poland, she worked as a clerk at the office of the municipality. She mastered English to a communicative level. But as she said, somewhere she got lost. The pursuit of money has always been the most important. She took all the overtime, to set aside as much money as possible.

For some time she was tired of monotonous work, lack of prospects, and above all the fact that everything seemed to her predictable. She knew what would be in a week, a month or even a year. Only the customers whom she cleaned for shifted. She was thirty-five years old then. Her husband also worked hard. Still they were not sure whether to return to Poland, or not.

I could understand that, but I would not be myself if I did not try to interfere. I immediately told her that the changes are good at any age, and it was time to look for another job – or at least to begin the search. We met at least once a week, and I always dug about. She could not determine a new perspective for her and her resume she perceived as: cleaning, cleaning, cleaning. That was the smallest problem, the biggest one was her approach. Finally, I managed to squeeze out of her what she was doing in Poland. During our meetings we were preparing a piece of SWOT analysis. In time, Danusia realised that some of her features and abilities were not extinct, she simply did not use them. It was nice to know that she had something to offer. After the fifth meeting she took the analysis home and completed it herself. She drew up a plan, not for five years but for two years. I helped her write the CV – it looked quite decent.

I sent her to a local agency Adecco. She arranged an appointment. We noted out everything she could tell in case she had questions about the sensitive period in her life – cleaning. She practiced the answers to basic questions normally asked during the interview. She was terribly stressed. I waited for her at the agency. I think everything went well because she was sweaty after the meeting, with her face flushed – but happy. During the interview at the agency she stressed she was looking for part-time work, and recruiters themselves admitted that in her case the best approach would be to work for a day or two a week, for different companies, thanks to which she would gain very quickly additional positions on her resume, as well as a new experience.

And so Danusia got her first job in sorting packages (for two days). Then one day she worked in a company entering personal data of customers. She was also employed in a pharmaceutical company at the adoption of goods, she spent two days at the reception, one day she received phone calls (this was quite a challenge), she also dealt with capitalisation of store cards for new customers. As you can see, she received job offers from various employers. She most liked her work at a school reception. They directed her there quite often because of different school celebrations, open days, meetings with parents. The receptionist employed there permanently was completing some courses and took a lot of days off. Danusia did not clean the whole week. At the end she received an offer for a permanent job at the school where she worked longer part-time, but this time at the position of an administrator with salary of £19,500. It was not much, but it meant everything. She immediately accepted the job. I will tell you that after half a year she was promoted to an Assistant to the Office Manager. Now, when I meet her, I see a completely different person. Satisfied with life, full of energy, she finally speaks about her work, because she has much to say. And of course, in the evenings she learns English in college.

If you allow, I will use the example of my younger daughter. She did not want to give up school, and at the same time she wanted to gain experience and earn her own money. She registered in a small, local employment agency with her humble CV. She named in it scrupulously all her positive qualities, based on school activities (she was in the last year of college), she enumerated other achievements, such as helping to organise open days of school. She indicated to the agency that she was looking for part-time work for a day, or a maximum of two days a week or on weekends. The first job she got after a week (office cleaning), and it was very close to home. She worked two days a week, for £7 per hour. I know, I know, you do not mean this kind of work, but you need get to know the agency, to gain trust of recruiters. After a month, she received a phone call asking if she could work at the front desk one day, this time in another company, receiving parcels and consignment and sorting them into different sections. The receptionist had a sick child. My daughter was offered a rate of £8 per hour. Of course she agreed.

Another job she took was for Vodafone. She was responsible for telephoning different people and verifying the information provided in the questionnaires. In the forms filled in by respondents some data was missing. The work turned out to be rather simple and easy – contrary to appearances, people willingly verified the missing data. After some time, she was asked to substitute at the reception, with a rate – NOTE! – £10 per hour. My daughter thought she misheard, but actually this much she was paid for each hour of work.

Since then, various employment agencies have contacted her with various job offers, usually for two or three days a week. From time to time she was also offered permanent jobs in the hope that, like other teenagers, she would abandon education in favour of a permanent job. Another job she performed on Saturdays, for charity, which dealt with the filing and registration of used furniture, knick-knacks, china and books. My daughter had to enter each item to register, determine the minimum price on the basis of the scheme and make a calculation of the value of items recorded and intended for sale. Quite a nice job, and one that looks good on your resume. It can even be seen as an introduction to a career in the finance industry.

Then my daughter found a job in a company that sold implants, as it was half-term, she accepted work for four days. She was responsible for sorting and preparing implants and other medical items for shipping.

The example of my younger daughter is the proof that lack of experience is not a barrier preventing from finding a job. In time, my daughter's CV has appreciated in value and is now already quite impressive. It is worth mentioning that she receives jobs mainly from one agency, which means that recruiters often get attached to their candidates who have a good reputation and fulfil in each role. Look for agencies working in the area of your residence or in smaller districts. Small businesses need employee to substitute every day and you need to use it.

Voluntary service

The next, perhaps the easiest way to find your dream job is to engage in activities for the charity sector. Of course, this is work without pay. You can do it once a week, on the day on which you have spare time. In this sector, an extra pair of hands is always needed, and the work can be very different: in a charity shop, in a warehouse (one of the activities of my daughters, exceptional rate), in organising meetings, preparing stalls, selling tickets, counting the profits from fund-raising . My colleague from the bank has done a lot of charity work, which I was surprised at, because she worked full-time. Twice a week, she organised a collection of used items (along with other volunteers) for a particular organisation, and in addition she helped charities in clearing accounts. Not only that, the girl devoted three weeks of her vacation and flew within a similar action to Uganda, to assist in the settlement of accounts, because as far as many people are happy to provide volunteering service in distant lands, so far very few people know the bookkeeping for charity. I was full of admiration for her, especially since she did not need this job to include in her CV.

You certainly do not have to go so far, just choose local organisations that will be happy to employ you. You can refer to your willingness to help, while also emphasising that such work provides you with experience which will help you in your career development. Perhaps one of you thought about working for a non-profit organisation (paid – which many people willingly decide on) and want to find out how these companies operate. You can also mention the desire to improve your language (as mentioned earlier, it is a priceless argument) and charity organisations usually depend on each pair of hands to work, and therefore the opportunity for employment is also for those who know little English. Make a list of local organisations and briefly write down what they do and for what kind of work they need volunteers.

Another place which allows for the start of a career in which, unfortunately, do not get a salary, but gain experience and the respect of society i.e. your future employers are food banks. They deal with the collection and sorting of packed food intended for the poorest. Such organisations not only need people to prepare food parcels, but also administrators, who will write down the gifts of food and distribute them to the package. The level of English language skills will have no significance in this case, and the experience gained while working in a team will count in the future.

Of course, there are various other organisations, for example those which take care of animals, where you can direct your steps. Benefits gained from working for a charity will always be mutual. In the UK this type of work is very respected. The employee gets the opportunity to do something good, and by the way they can gain varied experience, enrich their CV and, of course, brush up English.

Straight to the target

Being focused on your dream job, you can try right away to look for permanent employment. With a little luck, you can find a job. Let me give an example of my younger daughter again, who, tormented by me (my ambition has always been she would become a doctor or a dentist), organised within the required practice of school two weeks of unpaid work in a dental surgery. I was hoping she would convince herself to the profession. Unfortunately, she could not work any longer in the consulting room of a dentist's friend, because we moved out to the periphery of London, in the vicinity of Ascot.

I admit I did not have too much hope that after moving out my daughter would manage to find a job (I even felt guilty), but after visiting more than thirty offices finally she was called back by the three interested physicians. In one clinic they had a vacant post for a receptionist. It is not easy to find an experienced employee but my daughter already had practice in preparation of patient records and answering phones during the lunch break (paid work).

The second clinic was looking for a novice dental nurse. Probably the owner thought that my daughter was going to educate in this field in the future. Indeed, clinics often assist employees in career development and finance most of the courses. The daughter did not accept this job, because she had to hold a practice, not a permanent employment (about courses on dental nurse you will read later in the book).

My daughter chose the third clinic, which often employed students. Her decision was influenced by the convenient location of the clinic near our home. It was to be the work for free, as a part of school placements. Probably if the daughter was at a different stage of life, she would have accepted one of the paid jobs which offered her the owners of the remaining surgeries. Surely most of you would have done so. A dental nurse is a very good profession, where the rate after a year or two years is between £10 to £14 per hour, and after completion of the courses even more.

I will move back for a moment to the issue of seeking the first job by small local recruitment agencies. My daughter, of course, included in her CV a note concerning the practice in a dental surgery in the hope that the agency would find her locally an attractive part-time job, for example, on Saturday. To her and to my surprise, the agency three times offered her work in various surgeries in the position of a dental nurse, with access to training, but all offers related to permanent job, only one – four days a week. It was very tempting for her. My daughter wished she could take advantage of any of these proposals, especially that her friends were very jealous of tenders she received, but, well, studying is the most important.

There really is not a rigid rule on how to look for the first job in England. If you manage to take free practice in your chosen profession, I do not see obstacles against look for your dream job immediately after you finish practice. But do not limit the search to the area of your residence. Seek not only locally, but also in small towns and neighbourhoods. Moving does not necessarily mean disaster.

What is supposed to happen to a boy who is working on a construction site as a labourer or someone who is just taking their first steps in the construction industry? Without a good CV which contains a proven track of record of employment, a modest portfolio will be unable to convince potential English customers. Because all his time was spent on the co-creation of a project or he worked as an ordinary worker, although he has predispositions for painting and interior decorating. Certainly including in his resume such a position as a labourer is necessary. This is the starting point for him, to showcase his strengths, such as teamwork skills, accuracy, ingenuity. If you want to change your company and start looking for work in an English construction company or start your own business, you need to specify what you want to do. What are you the best at? After analysing, everything will become clear. Now you only miss a portfolio which proves that you are able to do the job which you are applying for (plumber, electrician, plaster, tiles, floors etc.) Do not write everything at once. Think about what you do best, and focus on this only. The next step will be to get involved in a small project. But how to get the first project?

Jacek had two colleagues who worked as helpers in one company. One of them could do plaster what he had learned while still in Poland (this skill looks great on your resume), and the other one, a car mechanic, wanted to lay wooden floors (and he successfully laid the floor in his apartment in Poland). In London, they worked as assistants, engaged in the carrying and unloading of construction materials. They were not allowed to do any other work, because they would constitute competition for the plasterer working there for three years, not to mention the carpenter, who had put floors in England for twenty-five years. They stood no chance. Both as a precaution created simple websites, which advertised their businesses and skills, but unfortunately without any photos. I suggested the following solution, which was initially ridiculed by their peers, much to Jacek's outrage. I advised that at the beginning they should do what they could do in their homes, or rather rooms, then take images of their work and put them on their websites. Photos before renovation and after renovation.

Well... I learned that not only would they work very hard for free, spend money on stuff but also would renovate two rooms for their landlords, what is more only partially because in one room would be done floor, and in the other one the walls. And how would they be able to put such pictures in the portfolio? The following day, I instructed them how they could go about it. They should renovate together both rooms: in one the guys put the floor and in the other they renewed the walls. Each of them would be able to include into their portfolio two projects, because the rooms were very different from each other. Of course, before I advised them to ask the homeowners if they would agree for free repair. They would be really foolish if they did not accept such a proposal. Both rooms demanded the overhaul, which was demonstrated in the pictures. To our surprise, one of the landlords in a gesture of gratitude, decided to give up two weeks' rent (nice one!).

To complete the portfolio they needed more demonstration work, I advised, therefore, that they both ask among their friends if anyone of them was planning a small repair. For sure there would be people who would be happy to save on labour costs. They did not seek for long. One of their friends wanted to renovate a room for their baby. The boys did it at cost. They were referred to other friends and in this way they earned some money. By the way, I will add that the other landlord, who did not feel to give even a symbolic payment for the renewal of the rented room, after a while turned to the guys asking to renovate his own home.

At the beginning the boys just wanted to find a job in an English firm in their professions. And it worked, they began to work for the Englishman, and thus honed their English. I do not know how many times they changed employers, but their portfolio grew, and free nights and weekends diminished for them. Now they are partners in a thriving construction company, hiring a plumber and electrician and construction helpers. There is only one conclusion: in order to reach the goal, you have to invest in yourself and demonstrate inventiveness – create your CV and portfolio from scratch.

In summary, at this stage your CV should present itself as it should be. No need to stress that in your application dominant unambitious positions because the skills you learned in every job can be useful in the following companies, and all previous work experience can be presented in a positive context and turn to your advantage. After including in the CV duties performed for charities and voluntary services and after adding a portfolio you can direct your career to the appropriate tracks.

Do not worry about building your CV based initially on odd jobs and small projects. The time will come that the same agency will begin to offer you jobs for longer periods, perhaps even permanently. Meanwhile, you do not have to resign from your current position and at the same time you gain experience with other employers.

I do not claim to know everything about job searching. Surely many of you have tried other notions about which I have no idea, and which look very cool. The beginnings are not easy, this is why I helped many people to prepare their CV, and advised them how to describe in the application successive stages of their career, which was sometimes enough to make a quantum leap on the way to the goal. One thing is certain: if you do not use ideas of people who succeeded, you will not be successful. You should draw inspiration from successful examples, the more that the impact of true stories usually works for others extremely motivating.

19
Popular ways to job search

If you do not want to do something, you will find an excuse.
If you want to do something, you will find a way.
Regina Brett

Local newspapers

The most common way of looking for a job is to browse the newspapers, especially local ones, especially in the beginning. Remember that you have to be careful and always tell your friends where you are going, for your own safety. Of course, you have to realise that a lot of people respond to such announcements, so it is important to create a clear CV adequate to the position you are applying for. It must meet all the requirements of the job advertisement and expose the skills and accomplishments which a specific company will benefit from, if you are employed in the offered position.

The newspaper *Metro*

A popular newspaper is the *Metro*, but of course you should be aware of its huge circulation. You need to stand out from the crowd with your CV.

On Mondays you can find here announcements from departments such as Public & Community, Education, Medical & Health, Building & Construction. As a rule, in the advertisements give an email address to which you should send your CV. Often, however, in small ads (especially in Building & Construction industry) there is a phone number only. I know from the experience of our friends working at construction sites, it is worth listing phone numbers of ads even if you are not looking for work at the moment. Ads are often posted by smaller companies, where staff turnover is high. Calling at such a number even two months after the notice may result in finding a job. As they say, you have to be in the right place at the right time. Of course, some telephone numbers may be temporarily disabled or no longer active. After half a year of writing down phone numbers you can get an idea of the frequency at which a company is looking for employees and whether still in the same profession.

On Tuesdays announcements appear of interest to people seeking employment in the following sectors: Office, Accounting, Hotel & Catering, Sales, Drivers & Riders, Education and Building & Construction. Most of Tuesday's announcements apply to employment in accounting. Various candidates are sought: both beginners and advanced ones. You should look at the job opportunities because they often contain a range of qualifications necessary to work for a given position. You can therefore determine basing on them what courses should be done to strengthen your position in the labour market.

Wednesday is the day on which jobs appear for sectors such as Media & Marketing, Building & Construction, Sales and Education.

Thursday is reserved for jobs in Social Care, Sales and Building & Construction.

Metro is a great tool to find a job, but definitely underrated. I will admit that I do not know too many people who found a job through this medium, but it is worth keeping in mind that it is an invaluable source of information. Almost every day of the week in the pages of newspapers information is published on employment in the so-called third sector (voluntary charity work) and offers of various courses and trainings. People taking the first steps on their career path, tearing up the treadmill of activities leading to nowhere, should very carefully write down the names of organisations recruiting volunteers. It is worth spending a day or two days a week on charity work, in order to acquire the desired skills and then include gained in this way professional experience to your CV.

Viewing ads gives a picture of the various positions and requirements for candidates applying jobs. Thanks to this newspaper I realised that to get my dream job – Senior Management Accountant – I should complete the courses ACCA (ACCA Fully Qualified) or at least complete a few exams (ACCA Part Qualified). That is why I found a university which provided graduates to obtain accreditation for this prestigious association. Having finished school, I had university degree as well as an international certificate of ACCA in my pocket, which I gained through successful completion of nine exams accredited by the organisation (I complete five more and I will be fully qualified). The name ACCA appears in most ads offering well-paid jobs.

It is especially worth reading those announcements for jobs that in the future you would like to apply for. You need to determine as soon as possible which courses you should enrol in and what qualifications to acquire in order to be eligible for attractive positions. For example, in the computer industry you can be a C++ programmer, in construction you should apply for a job as an electrician.

Surely most of you know that you can register on the *Metro* website and use the wizard CV.

http://londonjobs.metro.co.uk/

Other newspapers where you should register in search of work include the *Guardian*: http://jobs.theguardian.com/

and the *Telegraph*: https://jobs.telegraph.co.uk/

Job Centre

Many people register at the labour offices. I admit that I have never used their database. A long time ago I looked through vacancies published on their websites and came to the conclusion that very often the earnings were low there. Perhaps this was due to the fact that a company posting a notice in the Job Centre thinks (maybe wrongly) that most of the registered people are very desperate or hold poor qualifications or just need to be registered there to collect benefits. Of course I may be wrong, and my conclusions are based on the fact that none of my friends found work there. I admit, however, that many have benefited from the training courses organised by the Job Centre.

It is possible that at the time when you are reading my book, the situation has changed and is much easier to get a job through the Job Centre. Surely, you have friends who have tried to find employment in this way, perhaps with a very good effect.

On the other hand, job centres are mainly used by people, who do not really care about finding a job, on the completion of all necessary formalities. Therefore, if you include in your CV desirable qualifications and convincingly describe your advantages, it may be an advantage for an employer that you are Polish, as you are not just registered to claim benefits. A potential boss will appreciate that you are guided by different motives than just applying for free money. Thanks to my Polish origin I got my first job after University. I think that you have a good chance to be noticed by a potential employer.

20
Agencies. How to play with them

Courage is a state, when no one else knows you're scared.
Regina Brett

I hope that my experience in this field will be useful. Over the past seven years, many times I participated in interviews at employment agencies or directly with employers and thus I have mastered to perfection the game of the interview.

I have made contacts with recruiters, who now earnestly seek my favour, and meeting with them always results in obtaining employment. I worked for a long time for it to make recruitment agencies line up at my door, and not vice versa. They monitor the course of my career, to know as early as possible when my contract expires and that I will be active again in the labour market. Each of them wants to be the first to resume cooperation with me. Because of my experience I am a pretty good morsel for them. To achieve this, I devoted a lot of time and learned clever tricks.

The truth is that agencies earn good money from us, so if they see profit, they will not stop working with a potential candidate until they have been hired at the post from their base of offers.

At the beginning it is good to think about whether you want to work on a fixed-time, contract, or for a short period of time (temporary). For people who start looking for a job, I suggest not to be picky, because it really is irrelevant how long you are going to work for one of your first major employers. I think working for short terms or contracts will allow you to gain extensive experience in a number of institutions and companies, and in a fairly short time. I think it is really worth it.

On the other hand, if you are lucky and get a steady job, you will be able to enrich your skills and gain work experience in a linear and stable way, without the chaotic downtime on the job market. You should consider remaining in a company for more than two years. You will realise by then if you are making progress and whether you have qualified for promotion. It is also important to see how much of a raise you will receive after the first year – is it equal only the value of inflation? It is not worth to cling to the same company, because you end up spending time in a place where nothing is changing in your favour, and you at that time could earn more by learning new skills. As soon as you can, you should contact agencies to begin to look for something new. I decided to work in the contractual system, because I like to have an open road and the emergency exit. As you can see, even I sometimes have some concerns that are stuck in me somewhere deep. I prefer to have a short notice, so that, if necessary, I am able to leave if a position does not fit me perfectly. Luckily, I have not had to use this, but you never know.

Of course, the work on the contract has its drawbacks. Knowing that you are employed only for four or six months can be stressful for some people. There are longer contracts, nine or twelve months, which may suit you. It all depends on your preferences and financial situation. The good side is that because I am invited to interviews quite often, I always keep my CV up to date and I do not fall into a routine. Someone who decides to look for work on contract will attemd interviews two or three times a year on average. On the other hand, someone who wants to change their job after two years, it may find it stressful as they have not participated in an interview for a long time. This may exacerbate the fear of the unknown over changing work. People who have worked in the same company for a few years do not know how to convince themselves to change, and cannot imagine their first interview after so many years.

Another issue – on what basis do you want to be employed? If you work full-time, the company that employs you does everything for you; pays all fees and taxes, and your salary is determined by gross amount per year, just like in Poland. Usually after three months of trial there is three months' notice.

If you work on a contract or temporary system, you are employed by an agency within the PAYE and it pays all premiums for you and remuneration is calculated per hour, as a gross amount. In contrast, at the next stage it is required to have a Limited Company (LTD). Employees themselves are responsible for paying premiums and taxes, but rate per hour (or daily, if your career is advanced) is higher than in PAYE.* The decision is yours.

I must admit that when you begin working with agencies you should be flexible, and open to a variety of proposals that fit you, more or less. I mean, for example, longer commuting to work. Many times I was forced into a nightmare journey to the company office – long and with transfers. But it is worth it if your CV will be enriched by another impressive experience. When I was hired in the first major company, I had to go to work by bus and switch twice to a subway station. Nightmare. Even worse was when I worked on the island of Jersey. I was ready to live away from home (and family), just to pave the way for a career in banks. From today's perspective, I know that it was the best decision in my life.

Working outside London may also have its good sides. Such a job is often a lot less stressful. I know several people who proudly moved from the outskirts of London in to a bank in the City or to Canary Warf, and experienced a shock. The

---

* PAYE – Pay As You Earn system – a method of paying taxes in the UK. An employer deducts from your salary taxes and insurance contributions (in case full-time work). If the employer is a recruitment agency (for workers employed on a contract through an agency), it pays taxes for us.

pace of work in London is five times higher than in companies located outside the capital. These environments are completely different. That is right, the City is busy, but you get used to it, and the atmosphere which reigns here is unique.

Try not to stay long in one place. You get used to changes and will become hardened to working in different environments and with different people, at the same time providing yourself a frequent contact with employment agencies.

It is worth remembering that before hiring a candidate, agencies, at the request of employers, examine them in terms of good behaviour, and sometimes even check the state

of his or her finances. While smaller companies do not always do it, so much the banks forever. So let us take care of our finances: every six months check with Experian, which is your credit history. If you have any serious offence in your account, you can say goodbye to work in a bank. I mean, for example, not paying loans. Usually this control applies to addresses for the past five years and the period of holding particular bank account, but it can also be more detailed, even including a police interview.

The ability to 'crash' a recruitment agency will be extremely useful. You will think that it is very simple: you enter the site, register, create the wizard CV, submit your application and done! Starting from tomorrow they will ring with a thousand of jobs.

Nothing could be further from the truth. If you are born with a silver spoon in your mouth, they will call to you, but if you are not, you need to act. I know many people who, after a while after registration on the agency website, feel frustrated and resigned. They call me, saying that there is no work for them, that the agency is not interested in them because their CV is poor, that they are from Poland and they will not get their dream job.

And what, basically, have they done to get it? In what way are they different from other job seekers? Registration on the agency website and submitting a CV in a database is really nothing. I often ask if they apply for some positions at the agency site. Some people do not apply at all, because the most common jobs are inadequate for their experience described in the CV – they think, therefore, that it does not make any sense to apply for positions which requirements they do not meet.

The principle is simple: you have to catch an agent's attention! You have to remind them about yourself. Your beginnings will not be easy, but you have to learn to fight for yourself. No matter what stage of exploration you are at and how advanced you are in looking for work. You can set email notifications on each recruitment agency website. You will be informed by email about jobs which you are looking for as they appear on the database. Check daily email notifications about the ads. Do not limit yourself to only a few agencies. You can apply to all at your discretion. After some time, you will have your favourite offices. Of course, you have to come every day to their sites and send applications for various positions. Sometimes you need to modify your CV a little, but it is best to prepare them in advance, for example, for three different positions.

Why apply non-stop? Because behind every announcement may hide another agent. As you know, people are different. Some are more attached to work, others less. If you send your CV in response to two or three ads, it is possible that it reaches a maximum of two people involved in the same sector of the labour market. Applying for different offers will let more agents (in the same agency) hear about you, and there is a chance they will save your CV in their database for future use, if there is a position which can be applied for by candidates with less advanced skills and experience. From the beginning, I applied to hundreds of advertisements and I often received phone calls telling me that, unfortunately, my CV would not be considered in the recruitment process for a specific position, but be placed in a database for future use. Usually an agent asks us what kind of work we are looking for, what rate we are interested in and informs us about the potential opportunities for employment based on our CV. If he or she is not too brusque, ask what you can do to increase your chances and make your candidacy considered for one of the positions. Ask if they have any jobs for a minimum rate, which allow you to gain experience.

If, after a while, none of the agencies has called you, you have to make the first call. When you call, you should explain that you want to change the path of your career. Ask who you can talk about it, and ask to be put through to that person. You should write down the credentials of this person and in a few sentences explain what you have done so far. A recruiter will surely find your CV in the database, if you already have registered on the agency website, if not they will give you a personal email address to which you will send your application. If you are afraid you will not be able to put down correctly their email address over the phone (this happens to the best ones), give your email and ask the agent to send a blank message to you, and you respond to it, attaching your CV. Ask, what are your chances of obtaining a job and what positions, and if you need to modify your resume. Often, one agency has several offices scattered around London, so you should be in touch with each institution.

Another very important step in your job search is an appointment with an agent for a meeting. A little while after the first call you should call again and ask if there is a chance to meet, because you have more questions and you would like to talk about your career. Most agents will be happy to meet you, because they have to form the norm and hold meetings with both potential candidates and employers. This will have enormous significance, because agents like to see a particular person, often doing a brief description of the meeting.

Such a meeting usually takes thirty to forty minutes. You declare that you are looking for work on the contract of full-time. This gives you a chance to get to know two people from the agency, one of the department of full-time work and the other one – dedicated part-time work.

Once you get an invitation to a meeting you should bear in mind the famous saying: "Fine feathers make fine birds." You have to dress up and comb your hair perfectly, no matter what job you are seeking. Clothes should be appropriate to the situation – an elegant and sober outfit expresses respect for your interlocutor, and thus also for the employer. A classic suit or costume would do. Recruiters pay attention to dress and appearance, they usually wear suits and costumes, so arrival at a recruitment agency in jeans and sweater is a no no!

It is also worth calling about specific positions in order to be remembered. I know from experience that frequent phone calls to agencies move you to a higher position in the hierarchy of candidates. If someone is looking for a job, but does not call agencies they slowly become invisible. Recruiters may come to the conclusion that this person found a job (as a rule, people do not ring up all agencies to let them know this). If the candidate does not give any sign of life and contact with them dies, their CV is moved to the bottom of the pile of other applications. Candidates who storm the offices of agencies and are actively seeking employment, and who indicate that they are still in the labour market, are popular among recruiters. This information helps the agency to find a job for such a person. Often such issues prejudge the choice of the candidate.

When I was looking for work during my studies and after graduating from the university, I mastered to perfection the entire process described above. By being registered with about thirty agencies and by calling twice a week to each of them, I found myself after some time in the spotlight of recruiters, and my CV landed on the top of a sizable stack of applications. It came to the point that in the morning I received an offer for the same work from four different agencies. I worked out, therefore, the first line of attack. Of course, when choosing an offer it was decisive which agency sent me a notification first, but I also checked the amount of remuneration, as it happened that for the four agencies the rates were different. Sometimes I negotiated the rate with the agency I had chosen to represent me.

You should monitor any agency that organises 'open days' because during a meeting, you can get to know many agents, seek their advice and just be remembered by them. You can also go to any job fairs and collect contacts with more and more new agencies. Even the newly created are important because they will fight to gain clients in a fierce way, moreover the number of registered job applicants in an agency in the beginning will be small, so your chances increase. The new offices will want to satisfy candidates who were obtained with great difficulty. Of course, walking or calling an agency, you need to prepare yourself a few questions, practice them beforehand and use them during the conversation. Needless to say, your CV should be learned by heart.

If you get to the point where agencies will send you job offers to a specific position, you need to respond immediately to emails, expressing interest. Always in such situations, you should call the person who sent the notification. I know from experience that the same email may have been sent to ten or fifteen people. As I mentioned earlier, most candidates do not inform the agency when they are not looking for work, therefore recruiters are hoping that their email will be answered only by people interested in the position, those who are active in the labour market. The closer contact you will establish, the greater the chance that the client will receive your CV.

And the last matter – remuneration. If you are looking for a first job (for example, after cleaning homes of British employers or work on a construction site), do not try to negotiate rates. Take what is offered to you. I refer you to the chapter on CVs, in which I write about how to make your application more attractive. As previously mentioned, professional experience, which you describe in your CV, is crucial. Hence the idea of a voluntary or self-employment, since these forms of work are sometimes the only chance to make your CV more valuable.

When you have already passed the period of employment in several valuable positions, you can go ahead and negotiate your salary during talks with recruiters. If you talk to the employee of the agency which found the last work for you, you can negotiate the amount proposed, because the recruiter knows the rate at which you worked in previous jobs. You can rely on the fact that if you have already worked twice for the same rate, for example, £9 per hour, you already have richer experience. Even better when customers never complained about you and were quite satisfied with your work. There is a chance the agent will add £0.50, or even £1 to the offered daily rate. He or she just has to decrease their margin.

If the next role is offered by another agency, you can emphasise you are looking for work at £10.50 per hour, and if the agent asks about the rate which was offered to you in the previous company, answer truthfully – a little less. If you give a specific value, the agent will offer you the same salary. The point is not to lie to him or ask for ridiculous amount, but about making progress in the calculation of remuneration, so that with each post your wages will increase gradually, adequately to the growing experience, depending on the prestige of the position and degree of responsibility. What is more, you will feel satisfaction that your career is gradually evolving.

To sum up:

- Sign up at the recruitment agency website.
- Generate your CV or send it by an email.
- Call after two days, to see if recruiters have received your CV.
- Set the email notification of selected job offers.
- Apply daily for advertisements that appear on the pages of the agency.
- Find out what advice the agency offers on careers.
- Generate CV again weekly.
- Periodically (once or twice a week), call for specific recruiters to see if they have any suggestions for you.
- If your CV is unsatisfactory and agencies do not have for you now any offer, ask what you need to do to change it.
- Call to make an appointment.
- Do not be picky about commuting, even if the work is outside London.

- Negotiate the rate.
- Come to the open days to the career centres and job fairs.
- If you work on contract, and the date of its expiry is approaching, examine the structure of the company, if there is such a possibility you find you can apply for a job in another department. You can always send an email asking if they have a vacancy.

Many people who I have met on my way, call me and ask for recommendations to various agencies. If I know this person and the course of their professional history, I gladly give a recommendation. I know that it helps. I often mediated in talks between an agency and people who were looking for their first job, or wanted to change the job for a better one, but they feared of their poor fluency in English. There were a variety of industries, from hospitality, construction to banking. I am very happy to do it, if I have enough time or have a break between contracts.

On my website (www.career-24.co.uk) you have an option for asking questions addressed to me on recruitment agencies and many more. I am very happy to find out how I can help you.

21
Recruitment agencies and websites

*Life lies in the fact, to be in the right time there,
where you are expected.*
Regina Brett

For starters it is best is to look for simple work for which there is no need for specialised courses or high qualifications such as: Data Entry Clerk, Admin Clerk, Admin Assistant, Payroll Administrator, Accounts Payable Clerk. Also in other areas you will have to start from the beginning. Many agencies (eg. Reed) offer jobs for unskilled workers or helpers in various industries, not only in the construction sector.

For a career in the bank, you can start from the position of Front Office at one of the divisions of the institution. In this industry, they constantly look for assistants and staff who establish contact with clients immediately after entering the building and direct them to the appropriate window or show them things like how to use the machine receiving the cheques.

It is important to generate your CV every week, especially on such sites as Monster or City Jobs.

There are agencies which rarely offer jobs to beginners – they do not have a database of candidates for such positions – as they more frequently look for highly skilled employees. However, if a company needs a candidate for a lower position, it will return to the same agency, whose services they previously enjoyed. You should therefore be in a constant telephone contact with the admissions office staff. I am an IT professional, but by chance I registered in such an agency. It specialised in the computer industry and had in its database of highly skilled IT professionals. Several times a year, they send me job offers as an analyst, admittedly not in a bank, but in a very well-known institutions. They usually need great IT specialists, but if there is suddenly a vacant position in finance they automatically ask the same agency if they can recommend someone. And my CV is in their database.

Definitely it is worth calling to each of the recruitment agencies for advice on your career. Those who begin to search for and examine the market only should ask about any jobs that enrich their CV, i.e. positions for beginners (junior). If it happens that agencies provide a phone number to another office, which you do not know, they often deliver information about courses and trainings.

Below there is the list of agencies not only for beginners, but also for medium-level and more advanced candidates seeking employment (in the IT industry, web designers, etc.).

1. Accountancy Age Jobs
http://www.accountancyagejobs.com/
The financial sector, varying degrees of sophistication.

2. Language Matter
http://languagematters.broadbeantech.com/jobs/search/
The agency supporting almost all sectors of employment, offering employment for people who know a foreign language, both for full-time jobs and contract and temporary ones. If you know English well, you can find a job in the company, in which contacts in the Polish language will be required. I used the offer of this agency providing translations of interviews into the Polish language.

3. Reed
http://www.reed.co.uk/
Almost everyone is familiar with this agency, but not everybody makes use of its capabilities. It supports all sectors of employment

and it offers full-time jobs on contracts and temporary ones. It is worthwhile to register and set up an alert so that you will receive a daily email with job ads. It is best to stay in contact with several agencies, especially in your immediate area. By registering you will also receive other emails you may be interested in, including, for example, guidance on how to write a good CV, a list of companies that have made job offers on this day, positions for candidates with minimal experience. Some messages offer a list of paid courses that will help candidates find a job, for example, as an Administrator Assistant, Medical Secretary, Bookkeeper.

On the website there is a tab containing a list of free courses – it is worth reviewing. You will also receive emails with tips on building a career and a very helpful information on the topic: "What kind of work I perform."

I recommend this link:

http://www.reed.co.uk/career-advice/topics/what-job-can-i-do.

4. Walker Dendle

http://www.walkerdendle.co.uk/

Financial and technical sectors. This agency should be rung up, because job offers are not always posted on their website.

5. Robert Walters

http://www.robertwalters.co.uk/

Sectors: Accountancy & Finance, Banking & Financial Services, Human Resources, Information Technology, Legal, Tax.

6. Morgan McKinley

http://www.morganmckinley.co.uk/

Sectors: Accounting & Finance, Banking & Financial Services, Office Support, Information Technology, Human Resources, Tax.

7. Charles McKenzie Associates

http://www.cmrecruit.com/

Working mainly in the sectors Accounting & Finance (often offering positions for beginner candidates), for example: Administrator,

Ledger Clerk, Sales Clerk, Accounts Assistant, Billing, Credit Control Cashiering, Management Accountant, Financial Control.

8. Hudson
www.hudson.com
Sectors: Accounting & Finance, Banking, Office Support (Reception, Secretarial, Admin, Call Centre, Data / Entry Processing, Mail Room / Dispatch), Construction, Health, Human Resources, Technical / Operations & Engineering (Building Technology, Cabling, Design / CAD, Electrical, Maintenance, Security, Site Engineer), Sales, Marketing, Telecommunication.

9. Venn Group
http://www.venngroup.com/
They often offer trainee positions in various sectors: Accounting & Finance, Public Sector & Not for Profit, Health, Human Resources, Marketing & Communications, Housing (Housing Support Worker).

10. Real Staffing
http://www.realstaffing.com/en/
On the agency website there are often posted very attractive offers, but after you sign up for the agency, candidates receive automatically generated emails with invitations to work for beginners. Banking & Finance, Information Technology, Public Sector, Healthcare.

11. Contract Jobs
http://www.contractjobs.com/
A very wide range of sectors: Accounting, Administration, Advert / Media / Entertainment, Banking & Finance, Call Centre / Customer Service, Community & Sport, Consulting & Corporate Strategy, Education, Engineering, Healthcare & Medical, Hospitality & Tourism, HR / Recruitment, IT & Communications, Insurance & Pensions, Manufacturing Operations, Legal, Real Estate & Property, Retail & Consumer Products, Sales & Marketing, Science & Technology, Self-Employment, Trades & Services, Transport & Logistics.

12. Volt

http://www.volt.eu.com/

Sectors: Finance & Accounting, IT, Telecommunications, Life Sciences, Digital Entertainment, Engineering, Sales & Marketing.

13. JobsTheWord

http://www.jobstheword.co.uk/

Various sectors. It is best to register and forward your CV.

14. Badenoch & Clark

http: //www.badenoch&clark.com/

The agency often offers work for a very small rate, often for charitable organisations and volunteer centres. It is worth checking the site every day.

Sectors: Accounting & Finance, Banking & Financial Services, Human Resources, IT, Legal, Marketing & Communications, NHS, Public Sector, Housing & Charity Jobs (not for profit).

15. Page Personnel

http://www.pagepersonnel.co.uk

Supports not-for-profit sector. On the page you can find the contact to the various offices in different parts of the UK.

Sectors: Engineering & Manufacturing, Personal Assistants, Finance, Human Resources, Logistics, Paralegal, Public Sector & Not for Profit, Secretarial & Business Support, Sales.

16. Marks Sattin

http://www.markssattin.co.uk/

Sectors: Commerce & Industry, Corporate Finance, Management Consultancy, Taxation, Public Practice, Financial Services, Transactional & Part Qualified, Not for Profit, Internal Audit.

17. Hays

https://www.hays.co.uk/

A very wide range of sectors: Accountancy & Finance, Banking & Capital Markets, Call Centres, Construction & Property (Handyman,

Electrician) Education & Teaching (School Admin Jobs, Assistant), Energy, Oil & Gas, Engineering, Financial Services, Healthcare, Human Resources, IT (Security), Legal, Marketing, Office Administration (Customer Service, Administration), PA & Secretarial, Retail, Sales, Social Care (Support Worker), Tax & Treasury, Telecoms.

18. Robert Half

http://www.roberthalf.co.uk

Sectors: Finance & Accounting, IT, Office Administration, Secretary, Assistant, Customer Service, Personal Assistant, Administrator, Data Entry Clerk, Human Resources Administrator, Receptionist, Switchboard Operator, Team Assistant / Administrator, Telemarketer / Telesales.

19. Cameron Kennedy

http://www.cameronkennedy.com

This agency sometimes offers work for such positions as Junior Assistant or Administrator.

Sectors: Accountancy & Finance, Compliance, Commerce & Industry, IT, Marketing.

20. London Office Jobs

http://www.londonofficejobs.co.uk

A very wide range of jobs for everybody, at different levels.

Sectors: Accounting, Admin-Clerical, Banking, Construction, Consultant, Customer Service, Design, Education, Engineering, Entry Level, Finance, General Labour, Healthcare, Hospitality – Hotels, IT, Human Resources, Manufacturing, Management, Marketing, Non Profit / Social Services, Restaurant / Food Service, Retail, Sales, Secretarial, Skilled Labour, Training, Transportation.

21. Matchtech Group

http://www.matchtech.com/job/browse-jobs/

The agency offers a wide range of positions arranged alphabetically, from Construction, Data Analyst, Database Administrator, Food & Drink, Helpdesk, other very advanced positions.

22. Talent2

http://www.talent2.com/en_uk

The agency offers work all over the world: Asia, Australia, the United Arab Emirates.

Sectors: Banking & Financial Services, Commerce, Accounting & Finance, Construction & Engineering, Energy, Government, Human Resources, Industrial, Information & Communication Technologies, Insurance, Pensions & Funds Management, Legal, Manufacturing, Marketing & Sales, Mining & Resources, Office Support, Property, Public Relations / Communications, Retail Management, Sports Management, Supply Chain / Logistics, Technology, Tourism, Hospitality, Entertainment, Media.

23. Investigo

www.investigo.co.uk

Positions more advanced, but it is advisable to check every two weeks whether or not there are jobs for beginners.

Sectors: Accounting & Finance, Change, Strategy & Consulting, Front Office, Human Resources, Procurement, Property, Risk & Compliance, Supply Chain, SAP.

24. Aspect Finance

http://www.aspectfinance.com

The agency offers jobs for beginners. There are available very few offers on the website, you must register and call.

Accounts Assistant, Junior Account Assistant, Financial Controller, Client Accountant, Accounts Payable, Accounts Costs Accountant.

25. Advantage Resourcing

http://www.advantageresourcing.com

Agency has several departments. I would recommend Staffing.

Advantage Staffing – Administrative & Clerical, Skilled Trades, Industrial Light & Manufacturing, Construction, Call Centre, Hospitality, Distribution & Logistics, Retail.

Advantage Technical Resourcing – Project Managers, Software Developers, IT Operations Specialists, Mechanical Engineers, Construction Engineers.

Advantage Professional – Accounting & Finance, Banking & Financial Services, Executive Assistants & Business Support, Human Resources, Executive, Legal.

26. In-Pact Consulting
www.in-pact.co.uk

General Insurance – Customer Service / Telesales, Trainees / Graduates, Underwriters, Commercial Account Handlers, Claims (Commercial / Personal), Management / Executives.

Financial Services – Call Centre Staff, Analysts, Graduates / Trainees, Pensions Professionals (Junior Senior) Sales Support Administrators (IFA / Life Companies), Employee Benefit Administrators, Mortgage Administrators / Underwriters, Financial Advisers.

27. Ambition
http://www.ambition.co.uk
Admin & Office Support, Finance & Accounting, Financial Services, Sales, Marketing.

28. City Jobs
http://www.cityjobs.com
The whole range of jobs at entry level: Input Data Entry Clerk, Payroll Clerk, Administrator, Accounts Payable, Accounts Clerk Junior and many others, even with a rate of £1,000 a day (for gifted ones, unfortunately – who completed specialised courses). Sectors: Banking & Finance, Insurance & Financial Services, Accounting, Financial IT, Financial Marketing, Management & Executive.

29. Monster
http://www.monster.co.uk

Monster, similarly to Reed, has in its offer a wide range of sectors and positions at every level. Remember to generate your CV every week. Agents are always looking for new candidates who join the labour market. If your CV is in the database longer than a month, it may not appear in all search results. Usually CVs not older than a week are sought.

Sectors: Accounting & Finance, Administrative & Clerical, Building Construction & Skilled Trades, Business & Strategic Management, Creative & Design, Customer Support & Client Care Editorial & Writing, Engineering, Food Services & Hospitality, Human Resources, Installation, Maintenance & Repair IT & Software Development, Legal, Logistics & Transportation, Marketing & Product, Medical & Health, Production & Operations, Project & program Management, Quality Assurance & Safety, Sales & Business Development, Security & Protective Services, Training & Instruction.

30. Randstad

http://www.randstad.co.uk

Sectors: Contact Centre Solutions (Customer Service, Contact Centre), Care (Social Care, Allied Health, Nursing), Construction, Property & Engineering, Education, Financial & Professional (Banking, Accountancy & Finance & Legal), Business Support (Admin, Customer Service, Call Centres), Technologies, Marketing / Creative, Manufacturing & Logistics (Couriers, Freight, Warehousing), Inhouse Services, Sales, Retail (Store & Area Mgt., Head Office), Student & Worker Support (Tutors, Mentors, Notetakers), HR.

31. Change Group

http://www.thechangegroup.com

Work at all levels, from such positions as Sales Admin, Administration Assistant, Trainee Recruitment Consultant, Receptionist (they are sometimes looking for someone with the Polish language), and such, as Senior Manager, Sales Executive, and others.

The firm specialises in the following sectors: Accountancy & Finance, Hospitality & Catering, Office Support and Sales & Marketing.

32. Toner Graham
http://www.tonergraham.com
The firm specialises in the field of Accounting, from such levels as graduate through part qualified for the positions for the most skilled workers.

33. Orgtel
http://www.orgtel.com
For advanced. Asset / Wealth Management, Banking & Finance, Financial Consultancies, Financial Services, Financial Software Vendors, Insurances, Retail Finance & Retail Banking.

34. Evolve Recruitment
www.evolve-recruitment.com
They willingly give advice on careers. Sectors: Human Resources, Marketing, Languages, Sales, Oil & Gas, Finance, IT, Commercial.

35. CMC Consulting
http://www.cmcconsulting.co.uk/content_static/home.asp
Accounting / Finance (non-qualified), Banking & Financial Services, Industry & Commerce, The Public Sector / Not for Profit, Public Practice.

36. Sauce Recruitment
http://www.saucerecruitment.com
You must send them your CV and call. The agency has a lot of job offers for beginners. They willingly help candidates and give advice to applicants for employment.

37. Tricorn Selection
http://www.tricornselection.co.uk

The agency does not publish too many jobs on the website, but there are job advertisements for such positions as Accounts Payable and Clerk. Please send your CV by e-mail and stay in touch.

38. PCS
www.personalcareersolutions.co.uk
Please send your CV via the website.

39. Centre People
www.centrepeople.com
Register your CV – the agency offers work for beginners.

40. Accountancy Divisions
www.accountancydivisions.co.uk
As a rule, on the agency website there are not enough jobs. You must register and then call the agency and ask about the job.
Posts: Purchase Ledger, Sales Ledger, Accounts Assistant, Credit Controller, Payroll (these are the positions for Junior and Managerial).

41. Aston Carter
http://uk.astoncarter.com/
You need to register on the site.
Sectors: IT, Consulting, Financial Services.

42. Huxley
http://www.huxley.com
Banking & Capital Markets, Commodities, Asset Management, Insurance, Financial Services, Commercial Engineering, Supply Chain, IT.

43. Poolia
www.poolia.co.uk
Sectors: Banking Finance Recruitment, Banking Operations Recruitment, Accounting Recruitment, Finance Recruitment.

44. Goodman Masson

www.goodmanmasson.com

Banking & Financial Services, Business Change Management, Charities, Commerce & Industry, Energy & Commodities, Trading & Risk, Management Consultancy, Public Practice, Public Sector / NHS, Risk Management, Transaction Banking, Tax.

45. Eximius Group

http://www.eximiusgroup.com

Sectors: Finance, Operations, Technical, Law, Front Office.

46. JWC

www.jcwresourcing.com

Sectors: Retail Banking, Wholesale / Investment Banking, Management, Insurance, Oil & Gas, Minerals & Mining, Pharmaceutical.

47. Better Careers

http://www.bettercareers.co.uk

Sectors: IT & Communications, Engineering, Healthcare & Medical, Accounting, Administration, Advert / Media / Entertainment, Banking & Financial Services, Call Centre / Customer Service, Community & Sports, Construction, Education, Hospitality & Tourism, HR / Recruitment, Insurance , Legal, Manufacturing Operations, Mining / Oil / Gas, Real Estate & Property, Retail & Consumer Products, Sales & Marketing, Science & Technology, Self Employment, Trades & Services, Transport & Logistics.

48. Hyphen

http://www.hyphen.com

Please send your CV electronically, and vacancies are published on another page:

http://www.myfuturerole.com/employer/10016/hyphen/

Sectors: Accountancy & Finance, Agriculture, Fishing &

Forestry, Banking & Financial Services, Call Centre & Customer Service, Central Government, Charity & Not for Profit, Construction & Property, Education & Childcare, Engineering, Hospitality, Housing, Human Resources, Industrial & Manufacturing, IT, Legal, Manufacturing, Marketing & Communications, Medicine & Health, NHS, Office & Secretarial, Procurement & Supply Chain, Public Sector, Recruitment Sales, Retail, Sales, Science, Social Care, Sports Fitness & Beauty, Telecommunications, Transport Logistics, Travel, Leisure & Tourism.

49. HFG

http://www.hfg.co.uk

Register on the site, there are jobs for beginners.

Sectors: Actuarial, Audit, Catastrophe Risk & Exposure Management, Change, Claims, Compliance, Finance, Investment, Risk Management, Strategy, Technology, Underwriting & Broking.

50. Adecco

www.adecco.co.uk

The agency very often offers work for beginners, but it must be tortured with phone calls.

Sectors: Accountancy & Finance, Agriculture & Fishing, Banking & Financial Services, Charity & Not for Profit, Civil Engineering, Construction & Property, Creative, Design & Architecture, Defence, Education & Childcare, Energy, Engineering, Aerospace, Automotive, Hospitality, Tourism & Travel, IT, Industrial & Manufacturing, Legal, Management & Recruitment, Marketing & Advertising, Medical & Health, Office & Secretarial, Public Sector, Sales & Retail, Science, Sports, Fitness & Beauty, Transport & Logistics.

Once again, I remind you to:

- Sign up for the agency website
- Generate your CV or send your application by email

- Call after two days, to see if the agents have
received your CV
- Set an alert with notifications on selected offers
- Every day apply for vacancies that appear on
the agency website
- Check what kind of advice on careers
particular agency offers
- Generate your CV again weekly
- From time to time (once or twice a week), ring up
specific recruiters, to see if they have any offers for you
- If your CV is unsatisfactory for them and they do not
have any offer for you currently, ask what you need to
do to improve it
- Call regularly to make appointmentsDo not be picky
about commuting, even if the work is outside London
- Negotiate the rate
- Visit agencies on the open days and job fairs
- If you have a work contract, which expires soon,
explore the structure of the company, if there is such
a possibility it may be useful if you apply for a job in
another department; you can always send an email
asking for a free vacancy

22
How to write a CV

The wise continue to teach, fools know everything.
Apollinaris Despinoix

The internet is full of sites telling what form a CV should have. I know from my experience that the form is not so important. The most important is the information which you are going to include in your resume for the employer to notice your application. It is also important that your CV is universal – you probably agree with me that multiple redrafting CV for particular expectations of employers and positions for which you want to apply, would be very laborious. Therefore, I will show you my CV, and, for example, I will present a few applications of my friends.

While composing a CV, you should focus on acquired qualifications and education, your personal profile i.e. your acquired skills and positive qualities, and employment history. You must present the abilities through which you successfully carried out your duties in previous positions, and highlight character traits that will allow you to impeccably accomplish tasks assigned to a post for which you are applying now.

I present to you my CV:

CV number 1
Name: Ada Sytner
Address:
Mobile:
E-mail:
Date of Birth:

PROFESSIONAL PROFILE

Finance Analyst and Management Accountant. Budgeting and forecasting experience. Project and MI reporting skills. BA (Hons) degree in Accounting and Finance, ACCA part-qualified. Excellent management and stakeholders service skills. Ability to oversee several projects at once and to meet tight deadlines, a good eye for detail, work efficiently and effectively as a team member and without supervision.

EDUCATION

200X–200Y   Accounting and Finance BA (Hons) –
London South Bank University (3-Year course). Accounting, Financial Management and Control, Business Law, Taxation, Managing People.

199X–199Y   College of Computers –
Computer scientist Diploma (2-Years)

198X–199Y   High School in Poland with good A-level results

FINANCIAL EXPERIENCE

November 201X – May 201Y – XXX Bank, London
- Finance AnalRestructuring and designing finance department structure

- Creating and moving cost centres
- Involved in all systems changes
- Preparing Flash and MI reporting packs
- Responsible for Cost & Headcount numbers
- Investigation of reporting discrepancies
- Responsible for Cost packs
- Preparation of Corporate Card monthly reports

March 201X – October 201Y – XXX Corporate Banking, London
Business/Financial Analyst

- Responsible for monthly Management Accounts pack
- Responsible for workings for Income, Costs & BS
- Preparing analysis on Fees and Products
- Involved in analysis on reconciliation between MI and FI
- Preparing loans for refinance analysis
- Month end downloads and providing analysis on customer contacts & deposits
- Involved in a restructuring for Finance department
- Involved in template preparation

October 201X – February 201Y – XXX London
Finance Manager

- Designing and restructuring finance department
- Involved in budgeting and forecasting
- Responsible for the MI Board Pack
- Producing analysis on Income and Costs
- Preparing Forecast Trend file
- Executive Summary preparation – Revenue, Costs and Capital Funding,
- Responsible for RWA & Margin Waterfall

May 201X – October 201Y XXX – London
Decision Support Analyst

- Supporting internal changes to the planning processes
- Involved in creating templates for income and cost budget
- Testing the model to Identify risk and opportunities
- Supporting design and documentation of finance procedures
- Improve efficiency, control and cost reduction
- Responsible for weekly analysis of income
- Produce analysis on Project Portfolio
- Preparing 'Deferred fee' Report

October 201X – April 201Y YYY Bank – London
Assistant Finance Business Partner

- Provide financial control for direct costs
- Produce clear and effective monthly MI Reports
- Provide insightful commentary on current spend vs forecast for Direct Costs
- Collect information for costs and prepare spend report
- Attend forecasting meetings and daily month end calls
- Responsible direct costs and cost centre Accruals and journals
- Provide financial control and support for Projects
- Tracking spend, review and update at individual projects
- Review Project List on a regular basis

May 201X – September 201Y YYY Bank – Jersey
Management Accountant/Analyst

- Involved in budgeting and forecasting
- MI Reporting

- Preparation of Cost Tracking report
- Conduct financial cost-benefit analysis
- Preparation of Business Growth SPOT and Business Growth Average Reports
- Assisting with P&L commentary
- Balance Sheet reconciliation and control
- Monthly provision calculation report and analysis
- Preparation of all month end journals
- Trend analysis, analytical review and investigation system entries
- Query resolution on actual, budget and forecast for business partners

**February 200X – April 201Y – ZZZ Capital Partners Ltd
Assistant Financial Controller**

- Assisting Financial Controller in Management Accounting
- Preparation of Trial Balance
- Profit & Loss Account reconciliation
- Balance Sheet Accounts reconciliation
- Preparation of Monthly Group Management Accounts
- P & L year Forecast
- Cash Flow Forecast
- Intercompany Accounts reconciliation
- Fixed Assets and Leases reconciliation
- Preparation of monthly journals, accruals and prepayments
- Involved in preparation of quarterly VAT returns
- Processing of Direct Debit and Standing Orders payments daily
- Weekly Bank's reconciliation
- Sales and purchase ledger control

August 200X – December 200Y – WWW Ltd
Accounts Assistant

- Assisting in month end
- Trial balance and Intercompany reconciliation
- Preparation of monthly journals, accruals and leases
- Fixed assets reconciliation
- Involved in preparation of quarterly VAT returns
- Sales and purchase ledger control, ensuring correct posting of records
- Assisting and dealing with the Auditors by providing information and answers
- Processing and raising Purchase Orders
- Raising Sales Invoices and Credit Notes on a daily basis
- Control and updating on clients' contract and sponsorship agreements
- Processing and reporting on Depreciation
- Liaise with Credit Controller on any payments
- Credit Control responsibility for all Aged Debts
- Generating monthly Aged Debts reports
- Processing Direct Debit and Standing Orders payments daily
- Expenses payment runs
- Implementation of a new T&E Policy

Purchase Ledger Coordinator

- Coding and matching invoices received to PO's ensuring correct authorisation
- Insure all invoices are in line with SOX Policies
- Input of invoices into the SUN system
- Prepare Payment runs, Single HSBC Net Transfers and Cheque Runs
- Processing of Direct Debit and Standing Orders payments daily
- Bank's reconciliation at month end
- Responsible for ensuring remittance advices are sent to

- Checking and processing of associate expense claims in a timely and accurate manner through ADP Freedom

April 200X to August 200Y – VVV Ltd
Assistant to Company Secretary in Financial Department

- Assist the Company Secretary in order to meet all statutory requirements; this includes collation of board papers and contracts ratification
- Act as a point of contact for queries on Company cars, pensions, healthcare schemes, childcare vouchers, insurances, trademarks and data protection
- Administration of the Company car fleet through liaison with external providers and employees
- Administration of the Company pension plans and Company Healthcare Schemes
- Ensuring that returns are made to the Inland Revenue and to the Brokers/Insurers in order that legal requirements are met
- Ensure that costs are correctly allocated and are within the budget
- Complete P46 and P11D for all employees, who have benefits in kind

Computer knowledge:
Office Access, Power Point, Word, SAP System, Oracle, OFA, Khalix, Hyperion, Excel (advanced), SUN System

Languages:
English – Strong knowledge, Polish – Native language

My CV is quite impressive, but please note that this did not happen suddenly, in a few months. I worked hard for it, and I am still far behind other people who have reached a much higher position.

Below please find different examples of CVs, which are also useful for people who in Poland before emigrating, who have performed an ambitious profession but while in London must be satisfied with mundane task. The application should expose all your skills and achievements, regardless the positions you were previously employed. Of course, each of you will have to modify your CV to suit your needs, but I hope that the examples of my friends' resumes given below will aim you to the appropriate track. Note that the English language, which is used in them, is not perfect, but the documents are legible and understandable for the potential employer or agency.

CV number 2
Name
Address
Contact details

Education

199X – 199Y	**High School in Warsaw** – good A-levels results in Biology and History
200X – 200Y	**College of Economics** – Diploma in Economy (2-Years)

Skills and Knowledge
Organisation and communication skills

Working as an Office Assistant in Poland gave me the opportunity to develop my organisation skills. Every day I had to prioritise my tasks and that allowed me to meet all my deadlines. Also my communication skills improved significantly as I had to deal with management staff. As a Sales Assistant, I had to be an excellent communicator, dealing with variety of people.

Also working in London for English families, gave me the opportunity to communicate with different people, adults, children and elderly ones. Again I had to be very well organised to be able to finish all given duties on time, and organise my day between children play and housework. That also taught me patience and I had a chance to use my own *initiative*.

Reliability

Working in the coffee shop developed my customer service skills, time management and required responsibility when working on a till and preparing daily till reports.

My work as a childminder and housekeeper also required great responsibility as I was given keys and alarm codes. But the most important was the trust that the parents had in me, as carrying for young children is a very responsible job. But I always could win their trust.

Parents always had confidence in me, as they found me as an honest person who worked effectively and efficiently, with or without supervision.

Determination and motivation

I can say with confidence that I am a determined person. I decided to come to the UK and start my career from the beginning, not knowing the English language. I wanted to learn the language and develop new skills. My work history shows that I am a flexible person ready to take up new jobs and responsibilities no matter how trivial or hard they are. Even when I worked below my qualifications I always did my work up to high standards so my Clients were impressed with my work and I received very good references.

I am motivated, so I decided to work for Charity to develop new skills. My work for them gave me the exposure to different environment and to the real English language as I worked in a big team. They needed my help in every area, so I was responsible for administration, for orders, deliveries, and contacts with suppliers. I am ready for changes and challenges and I am going to carry on with my development in college.

Summary of Employment
Mar 2004 to Apr 2005
ADAX Ltd – Office Assistant, Warsaw

May 2005 to Sep 2006
Zax Ltd – Sales Assistant, Warsaw

Oct 2006 to Dec 2008
TYT Ltd – Office Coordinator, Warsaw

Jan 2009 to Jul 2010
Thomsons' family – Housekeeper, London

Aug 2010 to Sep 2011
Smiths' family – Childminder, London

Oct 2011 to Nov 2012
Costa Coffee Shop – sales assistant

Dec 2012 to Sep 2014
Gregs' family – Childminder and Housekeeper, London

OX Charity – Administrator, London

Interests
Bike riding, films, travel

References
On request

CV number 3
Name
Address
Contact details

Education
199X – 199Y High School in Warsaw –
good A-levels results in Maths and Geography

200X – 200Y College of Economics –
Diploma in Economy (2-Years)

200X – 200Y University of Lodz –
Bachelor Degree in IT

Organisation and communication skills
Working as an IT Assistant and IT Administrator in Poland gave me the opportunity to develop my organisation and communication skills. I had to deal with different people, help them to identify an issue with their computers and software and help them to resolve it over the phone. I had to be very well organised to maintain the log list with staff and clients complaints, as I had to response within the same day.

Also working as a labourer in Bristol, gave me the opportunity to work with skilled professionals and learn from them. I have gained new skills and trained my English. As a skilled labourer I had the chance to show my initiative and I could easily communicate with my workmates and clients. I was given more responsible tasks which proved that my manual skills developed significantly, and I was able to organise my day to finish all work on time.

Reliability
Working as an IT Network Engineer in Poland required advanced IT skills. I was responsible for computer network,

PCs and printers. I had to make sure that people could work on their desktops efficiently, and that all the issues had been resolved immediately. I had to keep all the information confidential and passwords secured.

When I worked as a Handyman my site managers had always confidence in me, as they found me as an honest person that worked effectively and efficiently, with or without supervision. Many times I was given additional responsibility as they had the trust in me. I was responsible for orders and deliveries.

Determination and motivation
I can say with confidence that I am a determined person. I decided to come to the UK and start my career from the beginning, knowing only basic English. I wanted to learn the language and develop new skills. My work history shows that I am a flexible person ready to take up new jobs and responsibilities no matter how trivial or different they are. Even when I worked below my qualification as a labourer, I always did my work up to the highest standards. My Clients were impressed with my work and I received very good references.

I am motivated, so I was able to convince my sites managers to use my IT engineer skills to set up computers and telephone network on a few sites. I did the set up with success. Since that time I have had to devote half of my time for the IT set up on every new building site, domestic and commercial. It was a huge step for me as I wanted to carry on with my IT tasks and I am happy to work for the construction industry developing new skills as well. My work for them gave me exposure to different environments and to the real English language as I worked in a big team of international workers. I am ready for changes and challenges as I know that I can work at a desk in the office and as a builder on the site as well.

Summary of Employment
Mar 2004 to Apr 2005
ADAX Ltd – IT Assistant, Warsaw

May 2005 to Sep 2006
Zax Ltd – IT Administrator, Warsaw

Oct 2006 to Dec 2008
TYT Ltd – IT Network Engineer, Warsaw

Jan 2009 to Aug 2009
Thomson & Son – General Labourer, Bristol

Aug 2009 to Sep 2010
BuildCom – Skilled Labourer, Bristol

Oct 2010 to Nov 2011
Contract Team – Skilled Labourer, London

Dec 2011 to Sep 2013
TTD Ltd – Handyman, London

Oct 2013 to Sep 2014
Sigma Ltd – Handyman/IT Engineer, London

Interests
Bike riding, films, travel

References
On request

CV number 4
Name
Address
Contact details

Professional profile
Very well organised, with excellent communication skills. Honest and reliable, work efficiently and effectively. Motivated and determined, with a positive "can-do" attitude. Able to work under own initiative in a stand-alone role. Strong IT skills, able to provide troubleshooting for both common and complex IT issues. Very good team player, with attention to details. Ready for the next challenge.

Education
199X – 199Y High School in Warsaw –
good A-levels results in Maths and Geography

200X – 200Y College of Economics –
Diploma in Economy (2-Years)

200X – 200Y University of Lodz –
Bachelor Degree in IT

Summary of Employment

Oct 20XX to Sep 20YY
Sigma Ltd – Handyman/IT Engineer, London
- installing pre-fabricated timber buildings such as stables, garages and garden rooms
- preparing first and second fix for electric work
- plastering and painting
- helping with joinery
- running cables for computer and telephone network
- maintaining all network and communication infrastructures

- providing IT troubleshooting support for software and hardware

Dec 20XX to Sep 20YY
TTD Ltd – Handyman, London

- assisting carpenter with kitchen units and door frames
- assisting roofing contractors – specifically sheet materials
- helping with bricklaying
- fencing and garden paving
- plastering

Oct 20XX to Nov 20YY
Contract Team – Skilled Labourer, London

- ripping out old bathroom and kitchen units
- assisting tradesmen fitting kitchens and bathrooms
- using all manner of power tools and hand tools safely and effectively
- assisting plumber
- painting interior and exterior walls

Aug 200X to Sep 20YY
BuildCom – Skilled Labourer, Bristol

- working alongside with a refurbishment team in occupied residential properties
- assisting tradesman
- operating power tools
- cutting concrete flooring and general site maintenance
- moving materials and tidying the site as required
- assisting flooring contractors

Jan 200X to Aug 200Y
Thomson & Son – General Labourer, Bristol

- general labouring duties
- helping fitters load/unload and fit products into residential properties
- helping with fencing, lawns and slabs
- lift furniture, wrap it and store it on a van for transportation
- clean contents on site
- pull up carpets

Oct 200X to Dec 200Y
TYT Ltd – IT Network Engineer, Warsaw

- setting up new team members and workstations with IT logins
- Overseeing and managing the required IT support for an office of around 40+ users
- assisting with the day to day management of the internal IT systems and help the end users with the system issues
- assisting with IT Projects – planning the stages of the project and monitoring how each affects the business
- ensuring relocated or new workstations are connected to relevant networks, and addressing any issues

May 200X to Sep 200Y
Zax Ltd – IT Administrator, Warsaw

- setting up new users and workstations
- providing day to day IT troubleshooting and IT desktop support for software and hardware
- assisting in maintaining all network and communication infrastructures

– understand and address end user problems, and assist
with solving issues that arise daily
– Implement improvements and safeguards into network

Mar 200X to Apr 200Y
ADAX Ltd – IT Assistant, Warsaw

– ensure the smooth running of the office
– responsible for administrative duties: telephone
answering, calls diverting and answering email
correspondence
– support internal IT systems
– liaising with suppliers of IT Equipment and Telecoms
– assisting with general office IT troubleshooting
regarding PC's, laptops, iPhones/iPads, email/
Microsoft Outlook queries, printing issues, internet
connectivity, network assistance, and Windows

Interests
Bike riding, films, travel

References
On request

CV number 5
Name
Address
Contact details

Professional profile
Excellent communication skills, well organised. Honest and reliable, work efficiently and effectively. Motivated and determined, with a positive „can-do" attitude. Able to work under own initiative in a stand-alone role. Very good team player, with attention to details. Ready for the next challenge.

Education
199X – 199Y High School in Warsaw –
good A-levels results in Maths and Geography

200X – 200Y College of Economics –
Diploma in Economy (2-Years)

200X – 200Y University of Lodz –
Bachelor Degree in Marketing

Summary of Employment

Oct 20XX to Sep 20YY OX
Charity Ltd – Administrator, London

- updating database, managing records and producing statistics
- taking inbound calls and dealing with customer
- generating reports and measures
- filing documents
- provide administrative support for other staff
- keep a log of current and future long term visiting workers

- responsible for monthly reconciliation of staff expense
- maintain notice boards and stationery stocks

Dec 20XX to Sep 20YY
Gregg's family – Childminder and Housekeeper, London

- grocery shopping and kitchen maintenance
- prepare weekly menus for family and guests
- occasionally prepare, cook and serve meals as required, including lunch and dinner
- ensuring children return safely home from school
- take children on outings and organise sleepovers
- ensuring rooms are cleaned to a high standard on a daily basis
- bed making, routine bedding and linen changes
- responsible for laundry and ironing
- feed & water cat and dogs
- responsible for monitoring all supplies and ordering of stock
- report any necessary maintenance work
- silver polishing
- oversee/supervise tradesmen/contractors if required
- packing principal bags when he goes away
- basic household bookkeeping
- adhoc babysitting

Oct 20XX to Nov 20YY
COSTA Coffee Shop – Sales assistant, London

- ordering goods and dealing with returns
- dealing with deliveries
- cashing up tills and banking money
- ensuring all food and hygiene standards are adhered to
- ensure all stock procedures are managed and controlled

within agreed targets and policies
- ensure the customer experience is consistently delivered by all members of the team throughout the store
- attend training and development sessions when required

Aug 200X to Sep 20YY
Smith's family – Housekeeper, Bristol

- food shopping, stock control and kitchen maintenance
- ensure home is kept clean to required standards
- preparation of breakfast on a daily basis
- preparing light meals occasionally
- maintaining the guest rooms, changing the beds, laundry of the bed linen and towels and some other laundry duties
- house hold plant care, watering some outside plants
- maintaining household inventory and security
- requisition and control supplies of cleaning materials

Jan 200X to Aug 200Y
Thomson's family – Childminder, Bristol

- accompany children to and from school
- helping with homework
- prepare meals for children
- preparing of school bags/clothes
- organising after school activities
- food shopping and kitchen maintenance
- maintaining children rooms, changing and laundry of the bed linen and towels
- minor cleaning and housekeeping, washing and ironing
- babysitting one night a week

Oct 200X to Dec 200Y
WWW Ltd – Sales Administrator, Warsaw

- answer incoming sales enquiries and direct calls
- liaising with customers/suppliers to resolve queries via phone and email
- prepare and send quotations and contract packs
- follow up on quotations
- inputting quotes and customer purchase orders and obtaining approvals
- creating customer invoices
- complete extended warranties contracts in a timely manner
- complete all required administration procedures
- provide support to colleagues as and when required
- manage stocking-in product deliveries
- obtaining shipping quotes
- updating in-house product data base with new and updated information
- manage monthly stock checks

May 200X to Sep 200Y
TED Ltd – Personal Assistant, Warsaw

- coordinate all work in the office and manage one office assistant
- answering telephones and managing director's calendar
- prioritisation, preparation and handling of correspondence, reports, circulars, minutes
- set up meetings, seminars and training
- assisting in presentations and preparing materials for slides
- managing stationary and equipment orders
- travel arrangements
- arranging Visa's payments

Mar 200X to Apr 200Y
BMC Ltd – Office Assistant, Warsaw

- ensure the smooth running of the office
- responsible for administrative duties: telephone answering, calls diverting and answering email correspondence
- support PA
- liaising with stationary suppliers
- assisting with general office inquires

Interests
Bike riding, films, travel

References
On request

23
Interview

You are born to win, but to be a winner,
you need to schedule a victory, prepare for victory
and expect victory.
Zig Ziglar

The key to success is, first – entering the labour market through employment agencies, relevantly presenting yourself and your strengths; secondly – an interview with a future employer. And here the secret is in skilful preparation for an interview. Because as long as good fluency in English is very important, the ability to answer questions in an appropriate manner is much more important. And this also can be learned. It is obvious that someone for whom English is the second language will not be able to respond eloquently to all questions in each area. This is impossible unless the conversation concerns a well-known topic. And that is the point. You really can perfectly prepare for an interview. It is a matter of training. The only way to master the art of self-presentation is speaking aloud, asking yourself over and over again prepared-in-advance questions and answers, and repeat them ad nauseam. If you group the questions according to several criteria, you may find that you really need to master only one answer to two or even three questions.

Bookshops are full of books with the sort of questions and answers which usually appear during the interview. Unfortunately, most of these publications are not very useful for people starting their career. The authors tell us to talk about our achievements and successes. Not only that, it would be good if we could determine how much time and money we have been able to save the company in which we worked. Having worked in most desirable positions, it would not have been so hard for us to prepare for an interview. It is easy to get employment on the basis of existing, significant achievements. What if none of us have them as yet? What examples to use during the conversation? How to convince our potential employer?

This book will help you prepare properly for the interview and succeed in it. I will try to provide you with my experience and help in answering questions which may seem on the surface make employers look down on novice candidates who are taking the first steps on the road to a career. You will learn how to promote yourself, and at the same time believe that you have a lot to offer to your new employer. Every company is looking for the same competencies in their employees, and all those qualities either you already possess or can develop them yourself.

The first step: Start by drawing up a list of responsibilities of previous jobs. Put your CV in front of you. In addition to even the smallest professional duties, list the qualities that allowed you to do the job – starting from employment in Poland to your stay in the UK.

The second step: Think what you would say about your achievements and your work to your current boss if you wanted to get a raise? How you would make such a request? What should he or she consider?

The third step: We all can solve problems. Think about what problems bothered you in the position you are analysing, the difficulties you struggled with to meet the needs of the employer, what challenges you had to face every day. Even if they were mundane, you should realise that the problems faced by you – whether with colleagues or work – in the end were resolved. What were the circumstances? What qualities, skills and competences did you manage to solve them with?

Write down your professional and unprofessional skills and qualities, thanks to which you were able to solve the problem. Was the solution worth it? What result did it bring?

At each interview, recruiters expect candidates to demonstrate their competence in this order: problem, solution, result. Do not worry if a problem has not been solved. Maybe now, years later, you come up with the idea to solve it? Maybe someone around you has solved a similar problem and following their example, you can use this knowledge in future work? Do not be afraid to tell an interviewer that that today you would solve the mentioned problem in a different way. It will prove about your maturity and the progress you have made since the previous position.

The fourth step: If in the previous workplaces you did not struggle with any problems, try to imagine what would happen if such situations arose? If all tasks had not been completed, it would certainly have had an impact on your work. What would have happened if the staff had not been punctual and responsible, and the procedure not respected? Probably it would have reflected on the results of the company. If you lack your own examples, you can always use events in the workplace of a friend. Introduce a problem which they faced and the approach your friend adopted. Do you agree with their solution? Define your point of view and the way you would approach the problem. This is important because if there was a similar situation in the new workplace, you will have a ready strategy for resolving the problem.

Interview

At the interview you must arrive early. It is best to know the way to the agreed place a day or two beforehand to make sure that you reach the company on time. Needless to say your breath should be fresh – therefore no event the day before the interview.

Remember that the person who conducts the interview usually was not prepared for this, to do it professionally, and they feel may awkward too. You must also be aware of the fact that the entire conversation will proceed to eliminate candidates who are not suitable for the position.

During the interview the recruiter will ask you various questions, wanting to test your confidence, composure and reflexes. They will want to check whether you have the desired (by all potential employers) features, and learn as much as possible about your skills.

Most employers will try to make sure that:

– You are able to perform the duties assigned to the position. Each of us possesses a combination of different skills that determine our ability and suitability for the job. You must prove that you are cut out for the job, citing previously executed jobs and experience you have acquired so far. Certainly professional – technical skills will (depending on position) will help, but they ultimately will not determine whether you get the job. You must prove that you are able to perform successfully any profession. If you worked in Poland in more ambitious positions, acquiring invaluable experience and your first job in England is physical work, retraining for the needs of the present occupation testifies on your behalf and proves your flexibility. It suggests that you can find yourself in all conditions. Professional behaviour in every position held and the skills and qualities that you have developed as a result of experience gained in the workplace are very important.

– You can work as a part of a team. This is a very desirable feature. Lack of understanding and cooperation in a team often results in delays and errors in the project. You must prove that every time when you were a member of a group or team, you constituted a very valuable item. And it does not matter whether you bring in an example from work, study or courses. It is important that without you the project, work or presentation would be imperfect because your contribution, commitment and synchronisation with the team contributed to the success.

– You are ready to take on additional challenges and take additional steps. You must be flexible and willing to perform different tasks, not just those provided in the specification for your position. Employers want to know whether, if necessary, you will make a cup of tea or coffee for the team, you will receive phone calls, jump out to fetch lunch for your workmates, or wash the dishes if necessary. This question is not meant to see if you are prepared to perform humiliating acts. This is in order to check whether you are the person who will do anything to help the team survive the crisis. You need to think about examples from previous jobs, even if it was, for example, cleaning. Have you ever performed a task that did not belong to your responsibilities? Have you picked up or taken care of laundry, sent a package or stayed longer to look after a child, because the employer stayed at work after hours? And while working on a construction site, have you not waited after hours for delivery? Have you not finished work for someone who got ill suddenly? Have you not sacrificed Sunday, because there was an unforeseen situation in the workplace? If you can present examples showing that in the previous work you showed involvement more than expected by your supervisor, a potential employer will immediately perceive in you a determined person who do their best i.e. an ideal employee who associates himself with the Company.

– It will be an honour to have you around. The employer will ask himself whether you will be easy to manage, if you are smart, if you have the ability to work with different people, at different levels, different ages, different religions, skin colours and with different disabilities, if you will be able to accept tips and constructive criticism, take the right direction in the time of crisis.

For the employer, it is important that the potential employee is able to synchronise with the team, will be tolerant of the opinions of others, or they will be an obstacle to the harmonious working of the group.

Your strengths

The next important issue is the preparation of a list of your strengths. Do not just list them, you have to be able to point out examples. Below I have included thirteen variations, but of course the list is longer – further examples append yourself. Do not forget to prove why you think you have them. In the following instances I will use the examples, which I and my friends use during an interview.

Positive traits/strengths – why do you think you have them?

– I am well organised

Jobs in Finance (regardless whether it is cleaning, financial analysis or sales) require good organisation. This is one of the most important skills, without which I would not be able to perform my duties properly. Every day I have to determine which activities are the priority, which is why I always do task-list for each day. I care about the order in files so that, if necessary, I can quickly find important documents or the data needed, and complete the task on time. My colleagues and managers who I worked with thought I was very well organised. Everything I did, I carried out in accordance with procedures, of which I was often the author. In a short time I was able to find important documents before staff meetings (find the lost item) and helped arrange a day plan during the crisis, and my work space is always neat and tidy.

– I have very good time management skills

I believe that I can perfectly manage my time. I can distinguish between the responsibilities that should be done immediately and those that can wait. The most urgent are located on the top of my list. I always keep deadlines and I often finish earlier tasks entrusted to me. I do not routinely have to stay after hours, which happens to some of my colleagues. When I have some free time, I willingly help others, because then I have an opportunity to learn new skills.

– I work effectively and efficiently

Getting involved in every job, and the project, I try to plan everything very carefully to finish the project on time. I care to include a lot of detail, data and information in documents, which transfers into high value of work done. At the same time I am a person who always looks for new and innovative ways to reduce the inefficiency and ineffectiveness.

– I always meet my deadlines

Deadlines (in any position) are very important. Thanks to my excellent organisation of work I always carry out tasks on time. In my previous post I had a lot of deadlines to meet every week (eg: materials to order, receiving goods from reparation, preparing invoices, their implementation on time, reports etc.), but I always performed the duties assigned for me within the given period.

– I have a good eye for details

My work required paying attention to detail. All tasks entrusted to me I carried out with care for their quality. I always checked very carefully, whether numbers served by me were correct. Each spreadsheet which I worked on had a built-in model to check if the calculations were correct. I would like to emphasise, too, that I have an eye for catching errors, therefore friends often asked me to check their calculations when they could not find any misconduct. (Examples can really be multiplied. Certainly when you have had to correct a job after someone has done it casually, especially if the employer was a perfectionist and demanded that everything was done/cleaned to perfection).

– I always work up to high standards

I always attach great importance to the quality of work and tasks. I try to be a perfectionist, so I make every effort to make my reports comprehensive. Still in college my presentations were often chosen as an example, and when working in groups, everyone wanted to be in my team, because working with me was the guarantee that our project would be unique and refined in detail. (Regardless the fact if you are a labourer at a construction site, or you work in a café, or you clean up, perfectionism is your ticket to a career. Employers are always looking for people who will not need to be watched, to do the work at the high level. Recommendations are confirmation that you pay attention to the quality of your work).

– I am a good team player
I am a very good member of the team, regardless the number of contributors. I am loved and treated with respect, because I am always happy to impart help to others, and my advice is constructive. I respect employees and their point of view. I am a naturally cheerful person, smiling, outgoing, which certainly facilitates communication.

– I have problem solving skills
Based on my experience, I can say that I have abilities to solve problems. Thanks to my analytical abilities I show the right approach to the problem and solve it in a few steps. At the beginning I try to look at the problem from a distance. Then I try to diagnose it and to determine all the factors that have an impact on it. I prepare a list of solutions, comparing the consequences and costs of each option to determine the best scenario. The last step is to present the problem to the employer and recommend the best solution. Of course, I ask my supervisor for advice.

– I am determined
I am a very determined person. If I take to something, I bring the project to an end. My determination shows in the fact that I decided to change the place of residence (emigration to another country), abandoning an existing well-paid job to start a new path of my career, gaining new and invaluable experience in the UK and improve my English. My determination is so great that I was ready to do work below my qualifications and start my career from scratch.

– I have good communication skills

Communication is the most important competence in the workplace. I realise that the exchange of information among employees, regardless of company, industry or position, is the key to success. Depending on the situation I convey information to my co-workers in different ways. This is usually in an informal, verbal way or by an email, but I always try to notify the team of any changes immediately. Also any changes about which other employees inform me, I implement immediately. Rapid flow of information makes it easier to complete projects and solve problems on time.

- I have analytical skills

My analytical skills are very high, which is why I decided to study finance. I like to analyse different scenarios, compare facts and figures. At each position on which I worked, I prepared reports which were very accurate and suggested a course of action, and the best solution for the company.

– I am motivated

I am motivated. I know my duties and I do them willingly. I can motivate myself. I am persistent in what I do, and I always finish the undertaken tasks, even if they are challenging. I do not give up easily and do not need support from others to motivate me to finish the job. Thanks to enthusiasm and passion I am able to motivate myself to achieve different objectives.

– I work well under pressure

I believe that in any profession, especially in finance, working under pressure is a standard. In companies where I was employed, very often there were situations demanding that I or the entire team worked under tremendous pressure to perform a project within the deadline. I can confidently say that pressure works for me stimulating and motivating. I believe that with proper planning and time management I can effectively reduce the panic which could possibly be accompanied by meeting deadlines on my schedule. I just do not let tasks entrusted to me to get out of control due to delays in their implementation.

– I am reliable

I am considered to be a sound and reliable person. The evidence of this is my punctuality, and the fact that the employer can always count on me in crisis situations (when I have to stay longer due to the receipt of goods or work on Sundays). My employers have always considered me as a very responsible person, delegating me – often as the only person from the team – specific tasks (request for looking after a small child, entrusting the keys to the house or to the place of construction, guarding goods).

All work teaches us many useful skills and develops our abilities. While working in various positions, you definitely learned time management, so that you performed work entrusted to you effectively. You always had to follow the rules and procedures, which meant that you were well organised. You often had to demonstrate creativity and initiative, to be able to solve unexpected problems. Looking for the first job in the UK, you had to be flexible and determined – after all, you started from scratch. Each position required from you some specific skills, but above all, honesty and diligence. I'm certain many employers appreciated your commitment, entrusting you more and more difficult and responsible tasks. The examples are as plentiful as the many Poles work in the UK. Of course, I am talking about people motivated and laborious. Probably many of you, working in a restaurant or coffee shop were trained for work or trained new employees. Perhaps you prepared daily fiscal reports or you calculated team working hours. You have a lot of strong features and you need to talk about them.

Going to an interview, of course, you have to know precisely the position which you are applying for, and know of what challenges are linked to the job. You must demonstrate that you have all the required qualifications for the job, which you will have checked many times in various positions and can solve problems. Say to them that on the first day of work you will be fully involved and without hesitation you will take to carrying out the duties entrusted to you.

Do not let yourself be surprised

Remember that if you have sent out a lot of CVs, you can expect a phone call, whether it is from a recruitment agency or an employer. You have to be ready for it.

I suggest you practice the interview with a potential employer by picking up the ringing receiver. It is natural that you will feel stressed with every phone call from an unknown number. It is important to control your emotions. Usually the caller asks if it is the right time to talk – you can still be at work and you will find it hard to talk about the new offer of employment in the presence of your current co-workers. Take advantage of this by saying that you can talk, but go to another room or that you have to close the door. You will gain a few seconds to calm down and reach for your CV, which you can peek at if necessary ("Yes I can talk, let me just close the door…").

Remember to smile (yes, on the phone) in order to change the timbre of your voice to a more friendly one. If you do not understand a question, ask them to repeat it. It is not a disgrace. After many years of work, I know that the British often do not understand each other and ask to repeat a statement. You can always put the blame on a bad line.

When an agency sends you to an interview, remember that even if the offered job does not seem attractive to you, or you are not sure whether you want to take it, do not give up on going to the interview. You will gain practice that will allow you to get used to interviews and answering recruiters' questions. I guess there is nothing more wonderful than going for an interview for a job which we do not care about. And approach it in this way – a zero stress. You do not want this job.

Also, if you do not understand a question, ask them to repeat it – it is not embarrassing, and you gain some time.

What to do if your statement meets opposition from the caller, they do not agree with you, or they call into question your position so you feel that the job passed you by? Do not panic. Remember that while arguing your opinion, you must be polite and calm. You will gain respect in the eyes of the caller if you show understanding for the other point of view ("I can appreciate your position ... I see your point ... I understand, of course ...").

And what if someone is looking for an employee with higher education? And you do not have a diploma? But you have experience! Calm down. If you have been invited for an interview (even though you do not have the proper education), it means that something in your application caught the attention of the caller – and this is your advantage. A recruiter probably assumed that you would be able to take the job offered and meet the challenge. You need to explain why you have gaps in your education – for example, you can say that circumstances have forced you to start making money as soon as possible, but thanks to that you have vast experience and comprehensive knowledge. Immediately use the opportunity to ask if the company motivates employees to development and trainings. Assure your prospective employer that you can now fill in the gaps in your education, and that you really care.

Gestures
We know not from today that the first impression is most lasting. While waiting in the lobby or at the front desk for a meeting with a recruiter, always smile and do not panic. I often happened to have been waiting for an interview with other candidates and I watched them studying their CV with panic. On the other hand, I try not to lose buoyancy, keep calm, maintain a positive attitude and do not give up the smile. I perceive every person walking towards me as a potential employer. Compared to people sitting next to me I look for someone positive and self-possessed. It really works. A recruiter, inviting you to a meeting, probably will approach toward you

and shake your hand, introducing themselves. Be nice, smiling and calm. It would be good if your hand was not cold as ice and sweaty. That means a big stress level.

You need to be aware that when you are under the influence of jitters and caught in the crossfire of questions, you lose control over your body. It is, therefore, worthwhile to train yourself answering questions in front of the mirror, because in this way you will realise how much you are gesturing and what you do with your legs. English is not our native language, so it is natural that while chatting we are gesticulating. I noticed that I do it routinely, therefore during an interview I must control it so as not to wave my hands too vigorously. Of course, you do not have to keep them under the table, but try to take control over your gestures. Sit back, you can cross your legs – it usually helps.

Eye contact is very important. Do not avoid it, but do not stare at your adversary without end. You should occasionally nod your head, confirming that you are following the course of speech of the interlocutor, and by saying: "Right." If the recruiter mentions something unique about the company or the offered position, you can say, "Really?" There is nothing wrong with having your CV infront of you to be able to look into the document. If you have references, you can take them with you to the meeting.

End of the interview
You must prepare questions which you can ask your interlocutor about the company and the position offered. You will show in this way interest and commitment (I will write about this in the next section).

If you are asked whether you want to add something, you can say that this work seems to you to be very interesting and that definitely you will bring in a lot of good to the company: "It sounds like a very interesting opportunity, I am sure I can definitely make a contribution."

24
Interview questions and answers

If there is one secret of success,
it is the ability to accept someone else's point of view
and looking from this perspective as easily as their own.
Henry Ford

I tried to group the questions so that you can use a single answer for several questions.

Fundamental questions asked during a job interview:

1. What do you know about our company?
2. Why do you want to work for this company?

If you know the company – it's half the battle. If not, well… you will not know anything about it until you glance at the website of the organisation. You do not have to study everything on it, it will be enough if you check what it does and how it works. You need to know what services and products it offers, whether it operates locally or globally. Maybe you're already using the service or product of this company? You can often read on the website what the organisation offers its employees, and not just about the social package, but also about career opportunities.

Answer: I know that the company has great products and services for individuals and business. I also believe that it creates a stable environment which provides training and professional development for employees who expect mentoring and opportunities for improvement. In addition, the company acquires more and more customers, expands distribution network and improves service for customers. I know that the main goal of the company is to become a recognisable brand, the best in the industry, and the most important thing for it is to maintain deep relationships with customers, employees and shareholders.

3. Please tell us something about yourself.

A very common question often asked at the opening interview. At the first glance, a very simple one, but don't be fooled by appearances. You need to focus on professional experience and values that make you a strong candidate for the position being offered. Don't make a mistake and don't tell in detail the story of your life. Focus on selling your skills and experience.

Answer 1: I'm thirty-seven years old. I studied Accounting & Finance at the University of London. As a student, I started working as an Assistant to a Company Secretary, and after graduation I worked as a Payable Clerk, Account Assistant, Assistant Credit Controller and Account Manager. My career has developed very quickly. The last post I was employed on was as a Finance Analyst, where the scope of my responsibilities was very large, therefore I had to demonstrate excellent work organisation and time management skills.

Answer 2: I have been a salesperson for five years with experience in various sectors: clothing, footwear and cosmetics. I was responsible for the receipt and ordering of goods, and as an exemplary employee I also dealt with the training of newly adopted people. I have great customer service skills and communication with employees skills.

Answer 3: For the past three years I worked as a nanny for two children aged three and five. I loved my job, thanks to it

I acquired many skills, such as creativity and patience. I am a communicative person, I spent a lot of time with children's parents, so I had to demonstrate the ability to listen carefully and submit to their demands. The art of time management I led to perfection, because I was also responsible for the preparation of meals and fine cleaning. I was given great confidence, my employers wanted me to live with them for a long time. However, after consideration of the proposal I decided on a career change, especially because my English is already on a communicative level.

4. How would you describe yourself?
Note: if it is not clearly defined what exactly the employer wants to know, focus on a professional career, mention two or three of your strong characteristics. You should include everything that is needed for the job.

Answer: I am a positive person who likes to work in a team. I am well organised, I work efficiently and with good time management I always keep my appointments. I am motivated and I like difficult challenges. I like to offer advice and assistance to colleagues. I also have a sense of humour and I like to socialise.

5. Tell us about the last position at which you were hired.
There is nothing tricky in this command. Just say about your last job, responsibilities and qualities that allowed you to fulfil them. Needless to say, you should emphasise everything that a potential employer wants to see in a future employee. Accentuate what is needed to take a new position. Everything is included in the job offer.

6. Why did you apply for this job?

7. What interested you the most in the offered position?

8. Why do you think you are suitable for this role?

9. What experience of working on a similar position do you have?

You should base on the job description contained in the job offer and compare it with the work done in Poland or the UK. You need to know what the similarities are and what duties will challenge you.

Answer 1: The job offer sounds very interesting, what is more, I believe that the new role is quite similar to my previous position. I believe that I have most skills expected by the employer, and the skills and knowledge needed to perform the new duties (mention the skills listed in the specification of the position that coincide with your experience gained in previous work). I read the job description very carefully and noticed that I will be entrusted new tasks, therefore I will have the opportunity to learn a new skills.

Answer 2: Based on the specifications of the position I realised that you are looking for a seller with customer service skills (or analytical skills), fit well in a team and responsible. I believe that the new role is a combination of responsibilities that I was doing, being employed in Poland and in my last job in London. I feel I have the necessary skills, so I am confident that I will bring a positive contribution to the company as a member of the team.

10. What do you expect from your new job?

Answer: First of all, I want to work with a company that offers its customers excellent service and products, and development for its employees. I want to use in the work my talents and experience (here specify what talents you want to use and which ones will be useful for the offered position). I'm looking for the new challenges that will allow me to contribute to the success of the team and the company.

11. What will you bring to the work on the offered position?

You can use the previous answer, adding that you will bring enthusiasm to the team, great organisation and humour.

12. Why did you leave your previous job?

Answer 1: I left my previous job because I was not able to grow professionally and the company was not stable. My salary was not adequate to my skills and contribution which I was bringing to the company.

Answer 2: One of the reasons for my resignation was a cumbersome way of working, but more important was that I did not have too many challenges, the company did not grow so I did not feel motivated. I would like to work in a prestigious organisation, which will provide me with the development and challenges.

13. What did you not like in your previous job?

You should not speak negatively about your previous work.

Answer: I must admit that I really liked the previous work but I felt that I missed the bigger challenges. As a result I decided to apply to this company because I believe that by working in your team, I will have more opportunities to demonstrate my skills and prove myself.

14. Has any of your previous roles been your dream job?

This question cannot be answered "Yes." It will mean that

the work you are applying for, is not your dream job and therefore you will not do your best, because you have burnt out and lost motivation.

Answer: I am proud of my work so far but I feel that the greatest challenges are still ahead of me. I'm still learning and gaining experience therefore I think each subsequent job at the moment is the best for me.

15. What are your short- and long-term goals?

16. What are your future goals?

17. Where do you see yourself in five years' time?

Answer 1: I think I should answer that question with a question. What opportunities can your company offer me? I must admit that if only it is possible and I will become accepted, I would like to work here as long as possible to enrich my professional experience. I hope that the company offers development for its employees.

Besides, I would like to finish the ACCA course. I only need to pass five exams to get full qualifications. In the future, when I have more experience and knowledge, I want to work on the position of Financial Controller.

Answer 2: I want to be a true professional and a valuable member of the team. From what I've heard, the company develops and xxx department requires the most attention, and I will do my best so that the company has achieved its objectives. I hope that by cooperating with my future manager, I will be able to develop. I have always felt that knowledge and experience open up new possibilities therefore for the moment I want to be a part of your team, and the future will show what other challenges arise in the organisation. I hope for a long cooperation and a wide range of responsibilities, because through this I will be able to grow and fulfil professionally.

18. What is your biggest achievement so far?

Answer: Although I think my biggest achievements are still ahead of me, I am proud of my involvement in the xxx company, where my contribution as a team member was huge.

I have learned there a lot (you can name a few acquired skills during that time). I hope challenges are waiting for me in the new job, thanks to which I will be able to boast even greater achievements.

19. Can you work under pressure and under stress?

20. What stresses you out?

21. How do you cope with stressful situations?

Answer: Stress is a part of everyday life, especially at work. Very often we undertake tasks that must be performed on time, or work in crisis situations where sometimes we have to stop the standard duties and perform additional work for our boss. Frequently extra tasks that we need to do are beyond our competence which makes us work under pressure. But it is quite normal because in each of my previous jobs there were such situations and I had to face them. I know I work well under pressure and in stressful situations. Stress is a motivator for me and motivates me to action. First of all, priorities must be set, what and in what order must be made to determine how the team can share the task, and when we lack manpower, we can always ask for help in another department which may just have free capacities

22. What are your strengths?

Answer: I am very well organised I know how to manage my time, thanks to which I work efficiently, effectively and always keep my appointments. I pay attention to details and my work always has high quality. I work perfectly as a team member.

23. What are your weaknesses?

You should assume that you have no weaknesses but starting a career, you cannot declare you do not have any. I do not think you should emphasise your flaws that could possibly influence on the position you are applying for. Try to draw attention of the interviewer to issues that still have no meaning for the job. So, the fact you have some flaws, will not affect the decision about your employment.

Answer: At the moment I do not recall any significant defects that would hinder my performance of professional duties in previous positions or my previous manager mentioned. Thinking about it now, I think my weakness is public speaking. I have no experience in delivering a presentation in front of a larger group of people, and certainly it is a skill that I should improve and practice, because I may someday find it useful. (At the end, if the interviewer is not official, you can point a trifle out with a smile.) I'm also not very confident because of my accent as English is my second language. I was not born here, so I still need to improve it. Thanks to it, however, I always try to make sure that I am properly understood. Communication in the team is the most important, thus I make every effort to ensure that everything works as it should work.

24. Describe a difficult problem you had to deal with.

25. Tell me about a difficult client who you were dealing with.

26. What did you do to show initiative?

It is difficult to recall instantly and identify problems encountered in previous companies.

It is good to consider before the interview what you were overwhelmed with at that time, what was a challenge you, what problems you hit and how you solved them. Maybe now you have another idea on how to deal with them?

Answer 1: In my previous job I happened to encounter a stressful situation where I had to react quickly. I was responsible for two children, one of them was only two years old. One evening, when I was alone with them (parents went out to friends'), she got a high fever. Unfortunately, I could not get in touch with their parents, so I called the NHS and was instructed to give the child antipyretic medicine. Fortunately, paracetamol for children was at home, so I could apply the sick girl the right dose. To my horror, after another hour the temperature rapidly increased, and I still could not get in touch with the parents. I gave the girl one more dose, but it seemed to me that the child had trouble breathing. I did not wait any longer. I recorded the parents of the sick baby a voicemail and called an ambulance, explaining the doctor on duty the whole situation. The child had the beginnings of pneumonia. The doctor said that I did the right thing as just applying the girl paracetamol would not help. It was necessary to give antibiotics. Her parents were able to listen to the message when they were on their way home. They apologised to me saying that they should have been in control of the phone and once in a while found a place within the range to see if there were any messages from me.

Answer 2: Some time ago I worked in a company that sold xxx. Goods sent daily reached our clients on the next day. But one day one of the recipients called with complaint that he had received goods inconsistent with the order. Having checked we found out he had been sent the order of another client by mistake. One employee called to apologise to the irate customer, however, he was very upset and rude. He announced that he would end his relationship with the company. I decided to call him and try to convince him to continue placing orders with our company. I called and very politely apologised to him, I asked if there had been many of this type of error? It turned out it was the first time during two years of cooperation. I asked if he would like to give us one more chance and I assured him the goods would be sent the same day by courier at our expense.

He was also offered a discount for that day's order and further orders. A discount, typically, we offered for orders over a certain amount, which this client did not reach. Once he agreed, the order with a discount was sent to him on the same day. Of course, I made sure to get in touch with the other client who fell victim of the same mistake and had not had time to make the complaint about the goods by that time.

27. Is it better for you to work by yourself or as a team member?

Answer: I do not know if I can give a clear answer to this question. I like to work alone, then I feel fully responsible for the project and I have to face the challenges. I know I do not need constant supervision, as independent work is very motivating and builds self-discipline. On the other hand, by working in a team, I have the chance to learn from other people, to use their knowledge and experience. In addition, a group can achieve more, learn new skills, learn to solve problems, share ideas. That's why I like to work in a group and I think it gives more benefits than working alone.

28. What should the ideal team be like?

Answer: I think the ideal team is a group whose members are helpful, friendly people, with great communication and a good work ethic. Each team member is really involved in the implementation of the project and respects the ideas and input of others. I believe that a good team works under low supervision and direction. And if there is a problem, it is identified and solved by the group. It is also important that people in the team had a sense of humour so the workplace is nice. I think that the job is easier when you have a lot of creative people around you.

29. What skills and values do you bring to the team?

Answer: I like to work in a group and as a member of the team I can contribute to joint projects their analytical abilities and problem solving and innovative ideas.

I always try to take care that the other team members are able to come to an agreement, and the work is done in time. My manager told me more than once that he was happy that I was in his team because I gave of myself a lot. Indeed, my colleagues can always rely on me and my contribution to the achievement of the objectives of the team is my priority. I am a person who does not give up easily when it comes to a new challenge. I am happy to undertake it after consultation with the team.

30. Tell me about a time when you inspired the team?

31. Describe something creative, what you did.

32. What did you do to show initiative and willingness to work?

Answer: I am a person who likes it when everything works fine. When our manager suddenly stopped appearing at work due to illness, the team was confused and our moods before the end of the month significantly deteriorated. There was a fear that employees without supervision would not fulfil their obligations, especially because the manager systematically checked our work very carefully and always reminded us of different deadlines, as if he thought that we did not remember them. I decided to act. I arranged a meeting and asked all my co-workers, raising their concerns and why they thought that our obligations would not be carried out without our manager. It turned out that our team was disorganised more by the lack of motivation than the inability to perform the tasks. I suggested that we nevertheless would try to do, as every month, our tasks, showing senior management that we were a great team and our manager that he did not need to control us so much. I established that twice a day we would meet at a five-minute meeting to see what progress we had made and if anyone needed help. The idea was great, because after a few days everybody each morning reported what they were going to do on that day, and brief meetings were an additional quality control on execution of tasks. The team ceased to stress, because everyone knew the duties of their colleagues and could count on help of others. Despite the tight deadlines we worked very well. The tasks planned for that month were completed in time, and our manager was proud of us.

33. Can you learn from disappointments?

Answer: I think that every disappointment must be treated as an experience that teaches us something. Of course, we have to realise what it was caused by, what mistakes we made and what we learnt from them. It is also important to leave the failure behind and do not think constantly about the disappointment because it would demotivate us.

34. What interests you outside of work?

35. What do you do in your spare time?
This question comes up in an interview very often and seemingly it is very simple. A potential employer believes that the employee who privately is committed to high challenges and plays sports will probably also achieve success in the workplace. According to most guides, employers are often impressed by the employee activity requiring cooperation in a group, because it proves that he/she will be compatible with teamwork. Especially they appreciate sports competition. Contrary to the recommendations I answer this question differently, trying to maintain credibility.

Answer: In my spare time I like active rest. I spend time on walks with the family, go to the cinema and practice jogging.

I try to take a break from work and recharge batteries before another busy week.

36. What does success mean to you?

Answer: Success for me is a job that I like and the team which I am in sync with. At work we spend a huge part of life therefore it is important for me to have a positive attitude to the place where I stay every day for many hours. Success is also being rewarded for my achievements that contribute to the company's achievements, as well as the recognition and respect of employees. Of course, money is also very important because it allows me to fulfil dreams.

37. What it is more important to you: money or a job that gives you satisfaction?

Answer: It is quite a difficult question, because both issues are very important. However, considering the fact that the work for more money may be incompatible with my interests and skills, I would probably prefer a job that gives me satisfaction and opportunities for development. It is important to do what you like and what you are qualified for.

38. What motivates you?

Answer: I am certainly motivated by work that leads to development. I like challenges therefore I always strive to take on new responsibilities. Of course, I will not lie that money does not motivate me because it is needed to fulfil dreams and pay bills.

I am also motivated by recognition and respect that my co-workers show me for a job well done.

39. How do you deal with routine and regular working hours?

Employers are aware that some people do not like routine tasks that are repeated ad nauseam, sometimes unfortunately every day. Also, regular working hours are not suitable for all people.

Answer: Regular working hours and constant responsibilities is what I am looking for. I am aware that the routine is needed in any job and I accept it. Most tasks usually are repeated every month or every week but it is helpful in organisation of work and planning when suddenly additional tasks emerge. I am sure that over time I will get more responsible tasks, which I will try to come to terms with my routine activities.

40. Why have you not worked for such a long time?
You must have a specific explanation of any interruption of work on your resume. Certainly you do not want the employer to have an impression that you are looking for any job just to make money.

If the break was not too long, you can try to distract the attention of the interviewer from this issue, saying:

Answer 1: I want the work to give me satisfaction which is why I decided to find a job where I want to settle permanently or for a long time. I do care that commuting does not take me more than forty-five minutes. My financial situation allowed me to look for a little longer. Therefore, it is very important for me to receive this job because I feel that it will give me the opportunity to develop and will allow me to gain rich experience. Moreover, access to the company is perfect.

If you've had a long break, the following answer certainly put you in a good light:

Answer 2: A person close to me in the family required a time of constant care so I and my husband decided that one of us would give up their job and take care of the sick person. My husband had just got a new, well-paid job therefore I decided to quit my work and look after the sick family member.

Now, this person no longer requires care and I want to go back to work as soon as possible because I feel that rested mentally. I am motivated and full of energy. (Childcare also can be included here.)

Answer 3: I understand your fears that I remained long without a job but I can assure you that I did not sit with folded hands – job searching is almost a full-time job. I spent plenty of time on registering in job agencies and attending initial interviews which they organised. When I realised that finding a suitable job would take longer than I thought, I decided to take up volunteering and it really made me hooked. But I care about continuation of the career on the position of xxx. As soon as there was a job advertisement in your company I immediately decided to apply.

Answer 4: Indeed, it is a long gap in my resume, but it is not caused by the lack of jobs. For a long time, I and my wife had intended to have the house renovated therefore when my last employment contract came to an end, I decided to devote my time to redecoration, since it had been put off for a very long time. The work was complex and took a lot of time and I had the opportunity to test myself in many areas. When the renovation was completed we left for a long, well-deserved vacation.

Now, I want to go back to work, to again be a part of the team.

Your questions to the person handling the interview

It is pretty important part of the interview. If you make a good impression on the interviewer, it would be good to show an even greater commitment and ask a few questions based on the information that you got during the conversation.

Why is the position available?

How many people have worked on this position in recent years?

Who will I report to?

Where will the work be located and will the traveling be required?

What will be my first task?

What are the opportunities of growth in the company?

Who is the biggest competition for the company?

How often does employee performance evaluation take place?

Summary
Often at the end of the interview an interviewer asks the candidate to sum up why he/she chose this, and not another offer. It is enough just to point out **that you have a good foundation from school/course and previously performed work, either in Poland or the UK, include similar responsibilities, therefore your experience will be very useful in the new workplace.**

Stress that you are **ambitious, you learn very quickly and looking at your CV, your career is growing fast, because you are open to new knowledge and experience. You always engage in what you are doing, you like challenges and working with people. You believe that you will be a valuable member of the team.**

If you are asked whether you want to add something, you can say that **this work seems to you to be very interesting and that definitely you will bring in a lot of good to the company "It sounds like a very interesting opportunity, I am sure I can definitely make a contribution."**

25
Two happinesses. Two daughters

*As long as you do not become who you want to be,
do not require the other to become the product
of your imagination.*
Thomas à Kempis

It will not be a surprise to you if I say that writing this book I had put off for a long time. I wanted proof that my foundations for work and the ideas that I will reveal to others have worked in practice. My friends and my family often use them.

Probably more than once while reading this book you thought that I was dictating to you what to do step by step, while I treat my own family leniently. As you have probably realised – nothing could be more wrong. My daughters also were under my pressure many times, same as Jacek, my partner. In fact, it was the pressure exerted involuntarily, flowing directly from particular experience, and not forced premeditated. My loved ones watched my struggle to overcome each successive stage on the road, which allowed me to be who I wanted to be – therefore they could draw conclusions from my determination. They have always been proud of me, but also admitted that sometimes they had doubts whether I aimed too high. They were full of fear I would get disappointed and lose motivation to climb up. Nevertheless, the whole family cheered me on the way to my goal. Jacek tried to keep up with me, and also to grow.

I admit I brought up my both daughters quite rigorously, but I always served them help and advice. They knew that no matter what happened, I would always be with them. Also, I was trying to convince them that there is not a situation without a way out and dreams impossible to fulfil. I often stressed that the choice of a profession is the most important decision in their lives. The best investment is to invest in oneself – in education and training, no matter the age.

Even before the GCSE exams I persuaded my daughter to focus on the study of science subjects, i.e. Biology, Chemistry, Physics and Mathematics. I argued for the professions of a doctor or dentist as professions providing financial security. They had a hard time with me. In my opinion, one could always be better. I justified myself by the fact that I was just as stringent for myself.

Both daughters hated Chemistry and Biology. At that time I got my first job with a daily rate – immediately after the contract at a bank in Jersey. I did not expect the elder daughter would fall for this reason in despair. When she found out how much I would earn a day, she burst into tears, saying that she would never be able to achieve as much as I did. She doubted her abilities. She claimed knowledge did not come so easily to her like me.

And then it occurred to me how much pressure they felt by observing how quickly I made my way to the top, which takes half a lifetime for most people. The elder daughter came to the conclusion that she would never go that far and would not be able to catch up with me. Then I told her very carefully that I started from scratch and how determined I had to be to get to the point where I found myself. I indicated I had not even dreamed of it. But she had a chance to jump me at least twice – she could graduate a decade earlier than I did. I am still a tangible proof that if you really want something, you can achieve this (even in your late thirties), but you have to work very hard and do everything in our power to achieve this goal, especially if acquiring knowledge comes to you with difficulty.

I admit that in high school, I was an average student.

My daughter probably realised the strength that came from my story. Sobbing, she said her English friends' mothers stayed at home or worked part-time, and when she told them her mother worked in a bank in the City, friends could not believe that, I being an 'elderly' woman decided to study and implement unimaginably arduous strategy, thanks to which I went so far. Well, 'elderly' – unfortunately, my daughters and their peers perceived me in this way. (I should disown them for it!)

To my surprise the girls passed the examination with science subjects at GCSE pretty well.

Time was passing by, but they were rather reluctant to study for exams too. Both Chemistry and Biology were problematic for my daughters. The girls blamed me, as I had exerted on them under pressure to take such difficult subjects. They claimed that they had no chance to be accepted to medicine. Even if they passed the exams, certainly they would not get an A, which guaranteed admission to medical schools in the UK. They could not imagine themselves in doctors' surgeries.

I heard it, I was obstinate and determined with action, but it did not mean that they were also such like. I heard again that they were not quite as smart or capable as I was.

Both daughters stated that they were unable to handle either medicine or dentistry… even for me. The younger daughter murmured something about Finance. I did not lose hope.

The younger one was seventeen, the older one eighteen years old. I thought that I still had some time.

In the end, it hit me that their assessment in Chemistry and Biology would not be sensational. Thus, they had no chance to enter a medical school in the first year. They would have to repeat the exams in two subjects to get better grades.

The elder daughter did not delude she would cope with this challenge. She could not specify what other field she might study. I must add that from time to time, she worked as a photographer for various artistic events with the participation of famous DJs, she even bought a professional camera with her own money. Her images were really appreciated, she got a lot of proposals for cooperation, but she did not perceive herself studying this field. Once she admitted she was very fond of assisting in the doctor's consulting room during her practice. And not once did she have a great desire to take doctor's tools and handle the patient herself.

I thought that I had to act. I had not spent so much time trying to persuade my daughter to become a doctor, to give up just now. In the end, we were earning with Jacek pretty good money. we had to make use of it. I kept telling my daughters I would willingly finance decent studies for them, for others unfortunately they would have to pay themselves – they would have to apply for a student loan. I did not know if that was the right move on my part, but both of them understood I wanted to reward their hardships, if they decided on such difficult study. I was ready to bear the financial consequences of our efforts to achieve the aim pursued.

I rang up all medical universities in Poland, with the program for foreigners wishing to study in the homeland of Chopin. I sent to universities documents and certificates of my elder daughter. The assessment of GCSE, especially the exams on Mathematics and Physics, in addition to Biology and Chemistry was decisive. She was accepted to dentistry in Wroclaw. Even I did not think she would be so happy. She did not want to believe me when I told her.

But after a few days, she began to cry and panic. She said it would be a waste of my money, because despite her best intentions she would not be able to cope with it, she was not gifted in science subjects, and learning rather came to her with difficulty. She argued that since she was not able to achieve very good results in examinations at A Level, the more she would not handle University. She felt sorry I believed in her so much, and she would soon terribly disappoint me.

A difficult conversation with my daughter awaited me. I decided to oppose her despair and panic with the arguments which were supposed to build up her self-confidence: "Any investment is a risk. And I take risk my entire life – and you are worth the risk. Everything is possible. There are no insurmountable barriers. Even if they exist, they lie only in our heads," I told her.

Sob. Sob… my daughter was implacable. It made me more reassure in the belief that it is worth making hay while the sun shines. We were both stubborn.

"If you have dreams, you must pursue them at all costs, and do not give up due to difficulties that may arise on your way," I continued undeterred. "Of course, it is related to enormity of work and sacrifices, but if these dreams are really important to us, we cannot retreat and give up. Do not be discouraged too quickly, no one said it would be easy. You have to keep trying. I also had the crisis in the second year…"

My daughter was weeping and weeping. She was very critical about herself. She was aware that she was a giddy person – as a rule, in her room there was always a mess. But I saw her in a different light. Always very popular with friends, she could take care of many things. She was not discouraged if there were complications, both at school and at work. And most importantly, she did not accept injustice, always in defence of the weaker or less resourceful. We often joked she would either become a lawyer, or a vendor. She argued about justice and was very spontaneous. Did she really believe she stood no chance? I wanted to shake her.

"Child, if I thought so, I would have never come to London. If once, when I was single with two young children, twenty-three years old, someone told me that I would work in a managerial position in Poland, would not have believed me. And if someone had told me that I would leave with the children for the UK and I would work in the heart of London, the City, earning a few hundred pounds a day, I would die laughing."

"Well, did you know from the start you would handle this?" – The daughter was unconvinced.

"In general, I did not know that I had such potential. How could I give up? At what point? Still in Poland, or already in

London? Was it difficult? Damned. Even extremely. Was it worth it? Do I not regret it? What shall I regret? The fact that we live in a beautiful spacious house, that I can fulfil our whims or I am willing to pay for your studies, that every weekend I can cultivate my own garden, plant trees and bushes? The only thing I regret is that I decided on this so late. Honey, one day you will laugh at your doubts of today. And you will be furious at yourself that it was a close shave and you would not try. And you might have let an amazing chance slip through your fingers."

Currently, my elder daughter is in the third year of dentistry. She went through the first and second year of study. I will not conceal she experienced moments of collapse. She called me buzzing that the exams were too often, questions quite different than anticipated, and that there were persons on her year to whom everything came easily. And I had to listen to this and support her. She often called five minutes before an unexpected meeting, which I had to prepare for. I reminded her about our conversations, when I was trying to convince her that it would be very hard, and she would cry, and I would tell her that it was meant to be. Because if medical studies were easy, we would have plenty of doctors. Fortunately, many people have found themselves in the same situation. Some came to study in Poland, because they lacked points to enter dentistry in their own countries. It was still easier for her. She studied in a country whose language she knew. Others had problems with communication, even in a store, not to mention renting an apartment. At least she avoided the stress arising from language barriers faced by almost all foreigners.

Her greatest problem was the lack of method and plan, according to which she could learn. But here her mates from the same year came with help. They were all in the same boat. They met in a group of a dozen people and studied together for exams. It helped her to deploy the routine and implement learning modes. She sometimes slept for an hour and a half. She fell asleep on the tram and woke up at the last stop. I knew she finally got a grip and did not want to disappoint me. But actually, she did not want to disappoint herself.

At the beginning of the second half of the first year he admitted to me that before Christmas she wanted to tell me that she no longer had the strength and I had better not pay money for the second semester. Because she could not cope with the onslaught of exams and tests.

Now everything has changed. The daughter came to the conclusion she had never studied so much. She had never supposed her brain could absorb so much information. And you can learn anything with a bit of practice. I think she will feel offended if I mention that she met her boyfriend on dentistry? Admittedly, he has German citizenship, but speaks Polish, because his parents also once emigrated to Germany to change their life, same as we emigrated to England. I like our Polish mentality. We Poles are a hearty people – and very persistent.

Congratulations, Malvina you won with yourself. This is your greatest success. Certainly, you will be happy reading these words. I know, I know, yet nearly three years to go.

You may ask: "What about your other daughter?"

Well… In this case the situation was more complicated. My younger daughter was not interested in dentistry, despite the practice she had at the doctor's surgery. She was making noises about studying psychology or finance. She had always been very stubborn and unruly, so it was difficult for me to talk with her about her plans for the future. Any talk about Uni ended in a quarrel. I tried to make her go to a medical school, as a dream field of study, she in turn, replied she would not be wasting six years – and subsequent ones for doing specialisation, because within a wink she would turn thirty, with life wasted on studying. The worst part was that – as befits the UK – most of her friends had long since said goodbye to education, taking a job –a better or worse one. Like the elder daughter, she also did not receive sensational results from Chemistry on her A Level, and she knew she had no chance to study medicine in the UK. Neither did she want to hear about studying in Poland. She was an Englishwoman, she spoke good English without an accent. She selected three universities, with the aim of studying finance, and there she sent applications.

I still did not lose hope. Although my daughters had completely different characters and often had arguments, when separated they longed for each other. The older one suggested that the younger sister should visit her and come to Wroclaw for a few days. It dawned on me. Great idea. Let her go and see the environment in which she eventually would come to live for quite a few years.

Indeed she returned happy, thrilled with older sister's books. She met her friends and she really liked Wroclaw. We were jumping out of joy. The younger daughter went there again. Unfortunately, after a while she categorically stated that dentistry is not for her. In addition, she was accepted to the dream (and quite good) University of Portsmouth, for finance. I thought it was a great option, but there is nothing to prevent her documents were also sent to universities in Poland. She agreed, just in case. I felt she was a little jealous of her sister who could cope well at such a difficult field of study. And it was Daria when she was younger who was interested in the *CSI* series and often said she would like to work in the lab, examining the evidence of the crime.

As I said, in July I started to assemble her documents for dentistry to Wroclaw and Daria at that time went on a visit to the dream University of Portsmouth. Soon it turned out we lacked a few GCSE certificates, and we had to apply for duplicates. I submitted the application in time, but because it was incomplete, it was not presented during the next committee meeting. In addition, the university was already overflowing with students in this faculty. I was told that I could look for more places in other cities. I could not believe it was over.

I told my daughter that she no longer had to stress herself out with the choice, because everything had just become clear. She was not accepted to dentistry. I thought Daria would be pleased, after all, she got her way... but she started to cry. I thought deep down she knew that this faculty was the right way, but her perverse nature made her want to study finance. She knew that she was losing something that not everyone is given. I was sorry I helped my elder daughter enter Wroclaw University, and in the case of the younger one I suffered a defeat.

I could not leave that just like that. There was one more chance – after all, dentistry accepts only about thirty people, but medicine – one hundred and twenty. On the same day I called the university, asking if they had already completed recruitment for medicine for English-speaking students. I was told that in two hours recruitment would be shut and basically they already had the set, but everything would be determined by the assessment and the number of examinations in science subjects taken at A Level. The Commission meeting was held the next morning.

I did not tell Daria I had submitted her documents for medicine. I preferred to wait for the decision of the committee. After two days I received an email stating that my daughter was accepted to Medical Faculty of the University of Wroclaw. Now I started to cry.

I told Daria that she was entered for medicine and, if she wanted, she could move to dentistry after one year, because the first-year subjects are similar. She had a choice. I saw she was happy. She called all her friends and in the evening she went out to meet them. When she told them she did not know what to do and what faculty to choose, everybody unanimously stated if they got such a chance from life, they would not hesitate at all. Finances was not an option when you entered medicine. I thought even my daughter was moved by the fact that a group of her friends – young people, who for various reasons had abandoned education – did not question the duration of studies and hardships of learning. Each of them would willingly risk if they got the chance. And the prospect of life without a student loan was promising. My daughter did not fail to mention that we would pay for her studies.

Daria is on the second year of medicine. She does not want to move to dentistry. Soon, some of her friends will fly to Wroclaw to visit her. She cannot wait. I was convinced that it was medicine that would interest her as a field of study. She was always very well organised, and her room was tidy. Pedantic pain, she liked to do her own thing, but I never had major problems with her. An Individualist. Very accurate. A lady pharmacist. The enormity of studying did not scare her at all. She did not pass one exam. It hurt her so much she swore she would retake it with one hundred percent assessment. She did very well. She says he will not give up.

I do not think I have to explain how much it means to me both my daughters study such in sensational faculties. The biggest dream of my life is fulfilled. I keep my fingers crossed for them, so that they will be able to finish their studies and overcome all obstacles.

I do not know whether they would have been motivated to study medicine if they had seen me or Jacek stuck in place and not developing. Children look at us as like in the picture and they need role models. Of course, I have no intention of interfering in your family matters and instructing you. Did I do the right thing by forcing my girls to start studying so hard? I do not even know if they will graduate. But I am proud of them because they have taken the challenge. If they complete University, they will be able to overcome all adversity. I am glad they are satisfied with their choice, they do not blame me for it, that I have fulfilled my personal dreams at their cost.

Sometimes it is worth converting our kids, not necessarily by choosing medical studies. Many children leave school after GSCE, having no idea for life. They work in various professions that are not at all the peak of their dreams, they often change them, which has a negative impact on their career.

Watch your children, whether they manifest interest in a particular field. It might be worth suggesting a child a course or participating in extracurricular activities. This will confirm whether your daughter or son has these, and not other, interests and abilities.

26
Website: www.career-24.co.uk

If you are interested in this book, I invite you to my website. (I'm working on it right now). If you are convinced that changing job is necessary, this site will, I am sure, help you edit and write properly a resume, regardless the profession you do. In the book, I included some examples of CV, of course, I will post even more of them on my website.

Every week on the site will appear more content that will surely prove to be helpful. If you happen to have any specific questions, for example about writing a CV for a specific job offer, please send me an email (ada.sytner@gmail.com) and I will try to post such a CV on my website. If you look for information about a course or training, please send your questions to my email – I will try to get more information. Similarly, in business matters: if you plan to set up a company, I will try to find information that can help you.

So far, I have had a lot of good, motivating information for you. Is there a catch? Probably not. I care to focus around my website people who are intensively seeking new opportunities, people who are determined for who it will matter that I will reply to their emails, I put specific information useful for most immigrants and English starting their career in the UK. Access to the site will be free. If you need one to one preparation for an interview, please send me an email.

I am sure many of you wonder why someone with a great job wants to engage in running a web page. The answer to this question is contained in the book. Since I can remember, I have always devoted time to this sort of advice. So, nothing will change in this regard. With the launch of the website more people will be able to benefit from my experience. My tips will serve a wider audience, not just my friends and acquaintances. I hope you find useful information on my website, not just abstract sentences that will not be helpful in your career change.

I am also thinking of launching an additional service to forward your CV to agencies that are looking for candidates for various positions, of course, with your consent. I keep getting

emails from head-hunters if I can recommend someone for a certain position, and I do not have any database. I do not want to waste time ringing up former and present friends, asking if they are looking for work in a particular industry. If it is launched, I will try to offer its users a wider platform to help prepare for an interview. You can already submit your interest by emailing me (ada.sytner@gmail.com) or in the future registering on the website www.career-24.co.uk (or polish web: www.kariera24.co.uk).

27
Summary

The luck you have to gamble,
for a Lady Fortune is not always at your side.
Those who never put themselves at risk,
they do not win the main rate.
Jacek Chmielnik

I hope that each of you will find in the book something for themselves. I wanted to have it both in a form of a biography and memoir, not just a boring guide. I hope I have achieved my goal.

Look carefully around each other – I am sure there not once appeared on your way a person who aroused your admiration and made you act. Maybe you were not persistent enough because you lacked vision.

While you were reading my book, perhaps it occurred to you that at every stage of my career I could stop and be satisfied with what I had already achieved. I believe that would be a great store manager, a qualified dental nurse or an accountant in my own company.

But it depends on you, when you want to start and finish a particular phase. It all depends on how determined you are and what you want to achieve.

I like it when people's dreams come true. Mine have come true. Sometimes in life you have to take the challenge and take the risk, overcome shyness, fear of failure or complexes resulting from poor language skills.

All obstacles are to overcome, and the stake is high. Just as in the song from a famous Polish movie *Vabank* – "Those who never put themselves at risk, they do not win the main rate."